891.66 DAN.

Print of a
Hare's Foot

Print of a Hare's Foot
Rhys Davies

An Autobiographical Beginning

Introduction by Simon Baker

seren

seren is the book imprint of
Poetry Wales Press Ltd,
Wyndham Street, Bridgend,
CF31 1EF, Wales

© The Estate of Rhys Davies
Introduction © Simon Baker, 1998

First published 1969
This edition published 1998

ISBN: 1-85411-180-9

A CIP record for this title is available from
the British Library

*The publisher acknowledges the financial support
of the Arts Council of Wales*

Printed in Plantin by
CPD Wales, Ebbw Vale

Contents

Introduction

Gwyn Jones once said that everything an author writes may be taken down and used in evidence against him. If so, Rhys Davies need not have worried. His autobiography reveals so little factually incriminating evidence about his life, that any prosecution would be doomed to failure. He had even dismissed the idea ten years before the actual publication:

> A letter this morn. asking if I could write my autobiography for a publisher. I'm replying that it would be too gloomy and that the truth (what use is such a book without the truth?) doesn't bear telling.

To say that the final product is economical with the truth would be an understatement. The original manuscripts reveal that he systematically rewrote the book in order to obscure rather than clarify the details of his life. There is no date of birth, no family background, no mention of brothers or sisters, nor education or personal relationships. It is a reticent masterpiece, largely devoid of dates, names and places. Davies teases the reader with a mock-manifesto in the opening chapter:

> Was it Taliesin who said that man is oldest when he is born, and grows younger and younger continually ... Did the poet mean that we grow younger through self-knowledge?

If writing *Print of a Hare's Foot* brought him such self-knowledge, then he trimmed it to suit his purposes. He rarely seeks to shed light on his life, especially his personal or emotional life. Yet these silences about family and relationships have a curious effect, invariably serving to intensify rather than obfuscate our interest. Perhaps this is because like all fine works of fiction they leave space for our imaginations to fill in the gaps. However, this leaves us with a problem. We still want to know something *definite*,

7

something *unequivocal* about the writer, or we wouldn't be reading his autobiography. In many ways reading this book is like reading poetry in translation. We know that we are only getting an approximation of the original, and it grates with us.

A part of the function of this introduction is thus revealed: to detail a few facts. Vivian Rees Davies was born 9th November, 1901 (not 1903, as he always claimed; and friends frequently called him Viv, although he preferred the more masculine Rhys). He lived most of his early years at 6 Clydach Road, Blaenclydach, and disliked later houses so much that he rarely mentioned them. His father was Thomas Rees Davies, an orphaned Grocer's boy from Tonypandy, and his mother Sarah Ann Lewis Davies, an uncertificated schoolteacher from Ynysybwl. They had six children, Gertie, Gladys, Peggy, Jack, Rhys and Lewis, although Jack was killed in the First World War aged 18 (another ominous and painful silence). Rhys left school in Porth aged 14, and worked in the Royal Stores for a while before moving on to a Potato and Corn Merchants in Cardiff, and a Men's Outfitters in London. His literary career encompassed nineteen novels, one autobiography, a biography of Danish adventurer Jorgen Jorgensen, two 'coffee-table' books on Wales, one produced play, a dozen or so poems, and over one hundred short stories. He listed his hobby in *Who's Who* as 'cultivating ruined characters', amongst whom were a variety of infamous Bloomsbury eccentrics such as Nina Hamnett, Anna Kavan and Count Potochi of Montalk. They had a tendency to perish and leave him money, so that he died a reasonably wealthy man on 21st August, 1978, having been awarded an O.B.E. ten years earlier.

Such, at least, is a bare outline of the known facts. His 'autobiographical beginning' suggests that he would have agreed with the Kierkegaardian proposition that we all live our lives forwards, but understand ourselves backwards: 'once more I knew we are always alone, and never bereft of identification with the endless past. Only the future was anonymous' (124). His childhood memories of the Clydach Vale 'shopocracy' abound with amusing stories and perceptive insights, as if we are watching his fictional characters reveal themselves in the flesh: 'I began to see almost everybody and everything as a potential subject for a story' (122). His domineering mother and her gossiping female customers became a rich seam of potential fiction, to be endlessly mined in later life. One obvious example (amongst many) is Mrs Hughes no. 8, and her 'eight tremendously eating sons ... "I've got eight men and a husband to feed"' (71-72), devouring bacon just like the 'big men' in 'Nightgown'. A picture emerges gradually of a self-conscious, distanced young man, waiting and watching rather than participating: 'I was not as bright as Idwal, though my eyes saw more than his' (39). His eye for the bizarre, the strange and the particular is increasingly evident: 'The preacher's denunciations and warnings were conveyed to me mostly by his facial contortions, and the tonal management of his thundering' (37), and his love of the eccentric and the loner, such as Dr William Price, an existential role-model who receives an entire chapter of perplexed fascination.

Part Two of the autobiography shifts its focus to post-war London:

> The Twenties, in hindsight the sunset close of an era, were not a conclusion then. They coruscated with intimations of complete personal liberty. It was the right age for rose-coloured spectacles.
> (101)

His dislocated existence as a young writer, an outsider moving from room to room, landlady to landlady, in a twilight metropolis of writers, artists, prostitutes and homosexuals, provided more fertile ground for his fictionalising imagination:

> Such bed-sitting rooms seemed damp from the tears of sad generations, [full of] keyhole spies, gifted with the baleful second sight and the ears of cats. Experts in the bestowal of humiliation.
> (114-115)

The forerunners of 'Boy with A Trumpet' and 'The Chosen One' can surely be heard in such descriptions. What cannot be heard, unless we listen carefully, is any discussion of his homosexuality. Only once or twice does it become overt, and then with a coy subtlety:

> Homosexuality — a term I did not know when I went to London — was not a thing to shut away. [On a friend who

had glandular injections as a cure] ... The result seemed
unfortunate. Previously a normal talker ... he developed a
bad stammer and twitched like a marionette.
(106)

Perhaps, as Eve Sedgewick argues, closetedness is a performance
initiated by the speech act of silence. Certainly Davies's friend-
ship with D.H. Lawrence circles around such sexual ambiguity,
the 'legendary figure bathed in messianic thunderlight' (127). His
insights into Lawrence are intriguing, the 'feminine sensibility ...
And did he, perhaps from some puritanic standpoint, watch its
temperature graph neurotically?' (139). Despite Lawrence's
dismissal of *Ulysses* as 'cerebral obscenity' (111), and Chekhov as
'a willy wet-leg' (134), Davies's 'carnal little stories' (112) were
significantly influenced by the older man, as was his outlook on
his profession: 'I had one of the loneliest jobs in the world. It was
also self-chosen' (183).

In curved space Davies arrives back at his departures at the end
of the book, back in Wales, only a much changed Wales by the
end of the 1930s, now more stale and uninteresting:

Each poky dwelling contained its thimbleful of dynamite,
at some time in the long boring years of obedience to
decent custom it would explode, and the moment of
explosion was the flower I sought. But there was a decline
and a diminishing now.
(176-177)

And on that despairing note, his autobiographical beginning
ends.

It may be that this appears a curious kind of recommendation
to read Rhys Davies's autobiography — by drawing attention to
so much impressionistic fiction, and so little hard fact. Maybe our
last question should be why he felt the need to write it at all?
Doubtless there were many reasons, but perhaps it gave him an
illusory sense of permanence and relief. Autobiography is surely
a means of retrieving, through a system controlled by memory
with the help of imagination, a past that, when it was actually
being lived, had all the appearance of chaos. Storytelling, fiction,
thrives on what real life — in all of its bewildering complexity and
unpredictability — inevitably lacks: a sense of order, of coherence,

of perspective. In order to understand who or what we are as individuals, and to determine the links between our actions and experiences, our only recourse is to come out of ourselves. With the help of memory and imagination, we throw ourselves into a world in which we are portrayed, paradoxically, as someone similar to, yet different from, our real selves. Fictionalised auto-biography like *Print of a Hare's Foot* is thus the complete 'being', a perfect blend of truth and falsehood; depicting us in our entirety, both who we are, and who we would like to be. In this it seems to me that Rhys Davies perfected every creative writer's challenge: to know someone for a lifetime, and yet ultimately to keep him a secret.

Simon Baker

Recommended Further Reading

Primary Works

Rhys Davies, *My Wales* (London: Jarrolds, 1937)

Rhys Davies, *The Story of Wales* (London: Collins, 1943)

Rhys Davies, *The Painted King* (London: Heinemann, 1954)

Rhys Davies, *The Collected Stories* (London: Heinemann, 1955)

Rhys Davies, *The Best of Rhys Davies* (Newton Abbot: David and Charles, 1979)

Rhys Davies, *The Collected Stories* (Llandysul: Gomer, 1996)

Rhys Davies Collection: Letters. Sterling Library, University of London.

Rhys Davies Collection: Manuscripts and Letters. National Library of Wales, Aberystwyth.

Secondary Works

R.L. Megroz, *Rhys Davies: A Critical Sketch* (London: Foyle, 1932)

David Rees, *Rhys Davies* (Cardiff: University Wales Press, 1975)

J. Lawrence Mitchell, 'Home and Abroad: The Dilemma of Rhys Davies', *Planet*, 70, 1988.

Dictionary of National Biography: Rhys Davies by David Callard (London, O.U.P., 1990).

Eve Sedgewick, *Epistemology of the Closet* (Harmondsworth: Penguin, 1990).

J. Lawrence Mitchell, 'I wish I had a trumpet: Rhys Davies and the Creative Impulse', in *Fire Green As Grass* ed. Belinda Humfrey (Llandysul: Gomer, 1995).

Sarah Mabbett, *Rhys Davies: Selected Letters* (Swansea: U.W. Swansea Library 1996. Unpub. Masters Dissertation.)

Rhys Davies, Interview with Glyn Jones, *New Welsh Review*, 35, 1997.

Part One

One: Flannel Shirt

This July morning, on my way to the market-place, I had paused for a moment to listen to snatches of song coming from an open window beyond a cottage garden overlooking the river on which fishermen's coracles could be seen. It was an old air I heard, vaguely familiar to me, but it was the quality of the woman's voice that arrested me. Contralto, running luscious as the juice of a dark plum, it was an untrained and effortless 'natural'. I caught a fleeting glimpse of the singer at an upstairs window as she shook out a duster. She looked one of those amiably blossomed wives with a pot-of-begonias chest; a good eater and, probable blemishes apart, a remover of irritants from domestic life.

Her song had the tones of melancholy that often haunt such native airs. Perhaps the fugitive snatches I heard prepared me for an unsealing of the past; sound is an ally of buried memory, though for me it has less reliable power to kindle the past than sight, scent and touch. And this town I was visiting, from London, lay within the province of my upbringing, though I was not a native of it.

Carmarthen, which I had always thought of as the cows' capital of Wales, still appeared to be prosperously lactic. The shire's milk-churns must have run into billions, their clanking sounding, in pre-lorry days, all the railroad way to London. My ancestors had lived in the deeper nooks of the restrainedly beautiful shire; it was 'the country' of my childhood ears, everlastingly green in my eyes, sweet-smelling in my broken nose. Born in a very different milieu, some seventy miles distant in the direction of Offa's Dyke, I used to think of the myriad teats squeezed twice a day by unworried women sitting on three-legged stools as they warbled to the sacred beasts it would go ill with us to lose.

I hadn't been back for many years. Carmarthen, a Roman military station in origin, of course did not live up to my romantic expectations. To look at, it had that utilitarian refusal to please the eye which is found too often in Welsh towns. But an attractive pastoral commerce was still to be found in the cheerful market hall. Wandering past the tables of robust poultry, dabs of farm butter, dense lard, cheeses, strong flowers, cockles, laverbread and the grossly fat lump of bacon called *cig moch*, I stopped before a more professional stall. This was heaped with rolls of locally-woven tweeds, bright-hued wool shawls, rugs and hefty blankets. I had noticed, with a far-away sense of panic, a single roll of flannel lying on a trestle table. Its thin rose and green stripes on a grey ground were familiar to me.

Long-ago winter Sundays came back, with their hurtling choirs of bitter winds and thrashing rains. True Welsh flannel was, and is, renowned for its warmth and tough endurance, and this roll of it on the stall was of the old hairy breed, woven probably in one of the few Towy mills remaining from the declined industry. While the stallkeeper, a gesticulating man in a bowler hat, talked in waterfall Welsh to a smart-looking woman who, a coiffured poodle under an arm, pondered over his blankets, I ran a finger along the roll of vividly striped flannel, and at the touch I shrank to the size of a boy of six or seven weeping in helpless protest against a dreaded Sunday morning ritual.

The sufferings of small boys, however puny the cause, are dense and permanent. Prior to divine worship in a Nonconformist chapel at 11 a.m. a shirt made of this same loathsome stuff was slipped on to my bathed flesh. The Sabbath change of shirt, following my weekly bathe, was a horror mainly because the fresh garment, by some vindictive alchemy of its washing a day or two before, carried extra crisp fire in its fangs; by the middle of the week the sweat-impregnated garment would lose much of this punishment. But also there was the victory of authority against my howling protest. Adult saints of the past endured a comparable martyrdom.

Such shirts were considered a safeguard against bronchitis, whooping cough and croup. Winters in our valley (it was the famous one-time El Dorado of the Rhondda) were mountainously full-sized. I remembered a belief among some colliers' wives that a trip through the long Severn tunnel, a suffering child's head pushed an inch or two out of the train window, cured bronchial ailments. I was never given such luxurious treatment. Flannel was my portion. The evil shirt slipped on by my mother's capable hands, something almost as tormenting followed. A neck contraption of cold, rigidly-starched linen, five inches deep and called an Eton collar (as a member of the lower middle class, I never wore the celluloid kind, which required no laundering) clamped my neck in halter discipline. Suit, stockings and boots were of lesser consequence and left no memory, except for a Little Lord Fauntleroy embarrassment of brown velvet tunic with a lace collar.

The stallkeeper's torrent of sales-talk Welsh to his lingering customer carried the same antique gallop as the chapel exposition of the Gospels that followed my manacling. Seated alone in my mother's rented pew in a Congregational chapel, I scarcely dared move within my hairshirt. To rise for the hymn-singing renewed the hot itching of my miserable flesh. Mr Walters's demoniac preaching, mounting into *hwyl*, sometimes brought forgetfulness. A good exponent of this chanting eloquence, he roared, thumped the pulpit-ledge, pointed an accusing finger at nastinesses down among us, thundering of our guilt. He placed a solid load of this mysterious guilt on my back, and I was suitably shirted to receive it. Unlike most preachers in the hundred or so other Rhondda chapels, who reserved their most powerful grenades for the evening crowds, Mr Walters had a perverse habit of giving his best performances in the sparsely-attended morning service. But the talent for *hwyl* in sweet, frock-coated Mr Walters — a childless married man, he much liked small boys on weekdays — was wasted on me as an aesthetic or theatrical pleasure. My shirt ruined all the blessings of religion too, its fangs mingling with the accusations of guilt. I would sit longing for Wednesday, by which time the malicious bites were lessened. By Saturday there was no torment at all. Then, next morning, my punishment began all over again.

Was it Taliesin, our sixth-century poet, who said that man is oldest when he is born and grows younger and younger continually? The miraculous product of the womb of Time certainly looks senile at its dropping. Did the poet mean that we grow younger through self-knowledge? Maturing age can at least bestow liberty. To be very young is not to be free. The worst period lies between, roughly, the ages of five and twelve. Before five a man is barbarously ancient, a creature of stomach and noise, a 'blind mouth'; after twelve he becomes, with dawning awareness of his emperor powers, a threat to his fellow creatures. Save for the interim period between five and twelve, Wordsworth's 'Shades of the prison house begin to close upon the growing boy', seems to me not true. But it took me a long time to get rid of those shades.

Two: Clydach Vale

Half-way up the main Rhondda Valley one of the tributary vales swerved away steeply from Tonypandy, rising for a couple of miles between reasonably attractive mountains. Clydach Vale was too steep for negotiation by the tramcars running through all the ten rude miles of the main valley, which finished beyond Treherbert, where beetling mountains closed round, and which opened at Pontypridd, a bustling town with a market day, busy police court and proper hotel where, as in England, bedrooms could be rented. Each of the other tributary vales running out of the Rhondda had its own colliery. Clydach was the one which had, at its high top reach, one of the big collieries of the Cambrian Combine, its fighting boss D.A. Thomas, the man who was to become Viscount Rhondda.

Cardiff, well-stocked with pale English people, lay a score of miles distant. The mining valleys streaking Glamorganshire behind the great port were not of good social and civic repute down there. In addition to the annoying strikes and constant industrial strife, rough men swept down from the mountains on Saturdays, especially on Rugby-match occasions, and roaringly made their presence known. Without those coal-rich valleys, however, Cardiff would have lain moping in an unimportant past and modern Wales have scarcely existed. Myopic journalists, especially in England, usually referred to these packed valleys as 'villages' and reached for such random words as 'grim'. The villagers of the Rhondda, and of its companion valley of Merthyr, in addition to breast-feeding the puling Socialist babe, enjoyed bi-annual visits by the Carl Rosa Opera long before the Kaiser's war, filling the plush seats of the Tonypandy Empire Theatre — a substantial edifice which stood next to a pioneering shop of Marks & Spencer and, past clanking tramcars, not far from Mr Ladd's photograph studio, with its camera on stilts, a black cloth over Ladd's head, and handsome scenery, palms and mansion chairs for displaying the sitter to elegant advantage. Indictable

19

murders were almost unknown in these seething 'villages'. Only wages and God were grim.

The Rhondda, because of its long size, fidgety population and battles for economic reform, was the best-known of all the wealth-producing districts lying among the hurl of mountains crowding the county's middle. Clydach Vale, like the other culs-de-sac running off the valley, was rough and well-behaved, religious and drunken, but never earned a nickname such as the vale that in due course was to be called Little Moscow. Lined with terraces and streets of standard dwellings all the way to the two-shafted Cambrian colliery, Clydach had a turbulent stream of mountain water changing at regular intervals from Cambrian black murk to a glassy purity of blue. The place gave birth to a champion boxer, preached magnificent sermons and, inescapably, it sang. I knew only one of its three hard-worked midwives — well-informed Mrs Bowen Small Bag, rightly a great gossip, who brought me expertly into the world while the new century was still taking stock of its advantages, and to whom I never thought of sending a bunch of flowers until too late. Like all the Rhondda, Clydach trumpeted an affirmation of the constructive urge in man.

In the last decade of Victoria's reign my optimistic father had opened a grocery shop in the centre of the vale's long main road and called it, for some far-fetched reason, Royal Stores. With several other shops, it stood opposite the Central, a massive pub of angry-red brick and dour stone which ran around its corner position to where a secret back door opened into an additional bar, an ill-lit cave exclusive to courageous women. A two-horse brake, its floor covered with straw in winter, stopped outside the Central at fixed times, plying from and to Tonypandy railway station with as many as eight passengers, its horses remaining alive until after the Kaiser's war, when a strong, single-deck bus appeared. A hansom cab could also be hired.

Within sight of my father's shop were two Welsh Nonconformist chapels, Noddfa and Libanus (there were five others up and down the vale), also St Thomas's church (English), a police station with cells for violent Saturday night men and rioters in strike time, and the Marxian Club (not called 'Marxist'). A doctor's surgery sent a warning smell out to the pavement night and day. There was a shop for locally slaughtered meat and one for ironmongery, flower-seed packets and punishment willow canes; also Ada Lloyd's shop for fruit and vegetables and, in her parlour behind hanging bunches of bananas, spiritualist seances; also a shop for sweets and ice-cream, kept by an Italian couple to whose daughter I suffered a token marriage; also Evans the Boot, selling what his nick-name implied; and Eynon's for moleskin pit trousers, singlets, buttons, American oilcloth, and 1s. 11^3/4d. per yard Welsh flannel out of which shirts and other distressing garments were made.

My favourite was the shop in which *The Magnet* and *The Gem* arrived efficiently on their proper day. I read everything coming my way, including my mother's *Home Companion* and *Weldon's*, finding cookery receipts and fashion notes almost as rewarding as Billy Bunter in *The Magnet* and — my father's slip of judgement — Horatio Bottomley's humbugs in *John Bull*. Fish and Penclawdd cockles arrived twice a week in a seaside-smelling donkey cart; and the Crier with his handbell stopped almost as regularly outside the Central to bawl announcement of some coming event. Of all the shops in the centre of Clydach Vale only the corner butcher's suffered wreckage in the riots and lootings that were to come; down in Tonypandy it was a different tale.

We lived for years behind and above our busy shop; a living-room, pantry and scullery behind, three bedrooms above. It was a 'credit' shop and a history of family fortunes. On a lectern desk panelled with a frosted glass screen lay an enormous black ledger, six inches thick, a double page for each customer. Its chronicle of strike-time debts was my mother's bible and bane, and in my mind it remained the Ledger of Old Accounts, durable as a lichened tombstone. My easy-going and popular father fed the multitudes in bad times; he also made some current money in good times. We could afford a domestic servant; Esther, the one I knew best and who stayed the longest, came from 'the country' like so many hopeful invaders of the Rhondda. We also kept a horse and cart, with a part-time man to drive them. A succession of schoolboys, together with my unpaid self, helped with menial jobs natural to our low status.

The shop smelled of wholesome things. Golden sawdust, thrown fresh every morning on the swept floor between the two long parallel counters, retained its breath of sawn trees. There was one chair, for stout old women panting on arrival from up or down hilly Clydach in our wonderful bad weather. There were lettered canisters of black and gold, an odorous coffee-grinding machine, mounds of yellow Canadian and pallid Caerphilly cheeses, rosy cuts of ham and bacon, wide slabs of butter cut by wire for the scales, and bladders of lard. Behind the counter over which my mother presided stretched wall-fixtures stacked with crimson packets of tea, blue satchels of sugar, vari-coloured bags of rice, dried fruits and peas, weighed and packaged by hand out of chests and canvas sacks on quiet Monday. Soaps gave their own clean smell, especially the favoured kind which arrived in long bars and, cut into segments, was used both for scrubbing houses and washing pit-dirt from colliers' backs and fronts. Slabs of rich cake lay in a glass case on an intersecting counter stacked with biscuit tins. Packets of Ringer's tobacco, black chewing shag, spices, almonds and dried herbs occupied a row of drawers under a counter, though not in the one always chosen by our cat for her frequent *accouchements*, filling me with wonder that she could force her heavy body through the narrow aperture at the back; an intelligent puss, she accepted the quick drowning of her load with experienced resignation and plodded on to the next adventure.

Down the backyard, which abutted on a rough lane such as ran behind all the streets, lay the stable of our horse, Tom. His tarpaulined cart stood, shafts down, in an adjoining space. They were used only on Fridays and Saturdays, a married milkman driving. Tom stopped unbidden at every customer's house; he knew them all. Mild in disposition, he liked to keep to a fixed schedule. Put out to graze in a pure field of clover and dandelions situated not far from disused coke ovens above the river, it was my custom to ride him there barebacked, and an unfailing custom of his, a moment before entering the choice pasture, to draw up rigidly and piss. I couldn't understand this regularity. My father had bought a trap secondhand from a bankrupt fellow tradesman, for occasional excursions into near-by rural parts on half-day closing and Sundays, and I never knew Tom to piss during these long trips, or on such delivery rounds as I accompanied on Saturdays; he reserved it then for the unharnessing on his return to the stable. He always chose the same spot outside the dandelion field and did not wait for me to dismount. If a woman happened to pass I was embarrassed. Was it the dashing sound of the nearby river that reminded him?

Our glossy trap made us seem stylishly well-off in comparison with nearly all the shop's customers. But my mother, who had been a trainee schoolteacher before marrying, kept an increasingly despairing eye on the Ledger of Old Accounts.

Sometimes she warningly curtailed the extravagant orders of families known to be feckless and drinkers. 'They've no shape in their ways,' she would discover, always unerringly, a woman with an instinctive sense of symmetry. Untainted by the romantic gullibility of my father, she swooped drastically now and again. Some particularly dodging family would find itself 'put into court'. This suit for recovery of debt usually followed news, gained invariably from her knowledgeable midwife friend, that the family had inherited a sum of money from an expired relative in the country. Such a family seldom paid up its old strike-time debt unless sued; and sometimes not even then. Hailing from a less raw and dangerous place than the Rhondda, it took my mother some time to subdue her puritanic irritation with the turbulent valley. But I was born into it.

Three: A Drop of Dew

Llantrisant was an easy drive in our trap. A hoary village crowning a steep green slope, it lay beyond a parting of the Rhondda mountains, not far from Pontypridd, the town where anarchical Dr William Price had earned notoriety in the Victorian age for some of his exploits, though it was at Llantrisant that he gained wider fame for burning the body of his infant son over a cask of oil. Llantrisant remained country for us. Blackberries could be picked there, cows stared at us from buttercup fields, and nobody, not even far-sighted Dr Price, could have foretold that when the twentieth century lumbered towards its last quarter the Royal Mint would plan to coin its money below the walled old village. In 1884 Dr Price had caused medals to be struck and sold there in commemoration of his pioneering cremation of his son.

As a knickerbockered boy, I always sat on the front seat of the trap with my father, my mother seated behind, a picnic hamper under us. I had not heard of Dr Price until one afternoon my father, while our horse trotted below high Llantrisant village, pointed his whip to a green eminence beyond and said to my mother, 'That's where they put up the pole for Dr Price, Sal. Sixty foot high and had a crescent moon nailed to the top. It was the spot where he had himself cremated after burning his little boy there'.

It looked an ordinary field, a few sheep recumbent on its gentle slope. My father said he had often seen the painted pole when he rode this way on horseback many years before. 'It used to sway,' he related, 'and one night it snapped in a big storm. I heard that twenty thousand people tried to climb up there to see the old rascal cremated.'

'Mrs Bowen told me one of his daughters is still living in their house in the village,' my mother said. 'I wonder is she the one he called the Countess of Glamorgan?'

'Better be called that than Jesus Christ,' my father commented. 'He named the son who died that.' I listened engrossed now.

'*Iesu Grist*,' my mother corrected. 'It doesn't sound so bad in Welsh. He was cranky altogether, so people expected anything from him. The last time I saw him was on Pontypridd railway station. He wore a whole fox-skin over his head, the tail down his back, and a green blouse loose over his red trousers. He had one of his little sons with him, dressed exactly the same. About fourteen I must have been then.'

'Well,' my father remarked, 'he looks cranky enough in that book by Morien you brought from Ynysybwl.' We trotted on towards Llanharran and picnic tea, with a white tablecloth spread on grass.

My mother was reared in Ynysybwl, a quiet village outside the Rhondda, but close to Pontypridd. She had often seen the mysterious Dr Price. Born in 1803, he had died in 1893, having become legendary in the valleys even before the famous cremations on the field called Caerlan. Many years were to pass before I delved fully into his antics. But when we reached home after the drive past Llantrisant I took a red-bound volume from a glass-fronted bookcase in our living-room and sat on the sofa. Of our two dozen books I had not looked into this one before. *History of Pontypridd and The Rhondda Valley*, by Morien (as the bardic author called himself) had not been a title to attract me.

There was a picture of Dr Price in the book. He sat on a garden bench, a bearded old man wearing his fox-skin head dress ('a symbol of healing', he called it) and a kimono and trousers with serrated ends. I did not know then that he bore a close resemblance to the aged Tolstoy. Cautious Morien had little to say about his scandalous contemporary. He merely remarked that Dr Price, at an annual druidic feast called 'Adonai', distributed cakes to people assembled before the prehistoric Rocking Stone on Pontypridd Common. But later I picked up word-of-mouth memories of the troublesome pagan and rebel, and later still ferreted other material in Cardiff, the British Museum and the Welsh bookshop of my friend Will Griffiths in London.

Dr William Price carried a history of the old Rhondda in his own life. He had all but seen his century through, expiring in his ninetieth year after drinking a glass of champagne, his favourite beverage all his debt-ridden life. Son of an ordained priest and Master of Arts living in adjacent Monmouthshire, he attended a school at Machen and then lived for five years with a Caerphilly doctor as a kind of apprentice. At home this offspring of a respected priest had already upset the neighbourhood by his habit of sunbathing in the nude on a hillside in full view of the village. From Caerphilly he went to London, and the Royal College of Surgeons found that the hard-working and penurious student passed all the examinations within twelve months. He qualified in 1821 and after further experience as an assistant in London returned to Wales and established a practice in Pontypridd.

'The sooty nose of King Coal,' as Morien called it, had already been pushed into the verdant Rhondda; and up in the neighbouring Merthyr areas the despotic ironmasters were in full reign. It was a kingdom the visiting Carlyle was to call 'a vision of hell'. It was also a kingdom created for the indignant exercise of Dr Price's socialistic and other beliefs. Surprised Rhondda farmers and rustic landowners had been disposing of their lands to bargaining capitalists from elsewhere; one of them had leased all the fabulously rich minerals under his feet for a term of ninety-nine years for £30 per annum and six horse-loads of coal per week. To house the streams of work-people trekking to this new cornucopia, blocks of dwellings were quickly built in dismal uniformity, public house and Nonconformist chapels breaking the monotony of the packed rows stretching from belching pits and ripped fields of iron ore.

Dr Price closely watched these developments. It seemed to him that the race of workers occupying the valleys, arrived mostly from pastoral areas of Wales, was in danger of developing wrongly. Their ill-organized but furious strikes for better pay and conditions kept a rough idealism glowing in their hearts, but there was a threat of complete demoralization by the new industrial age. These workers might rapidly lose their old racial integrity and their heritage of myth, legend, poetic gaiety and personal liberty.

Initially, the seer sought to bring back the spirit of an ancient, half-forgotten poetry. Tradition connected the Rocking Stone on rugged Pontypridd Common with the druids. On moonlit Sunday evenings up there, while the chapels below preached their doctrine to congregations groaning in a sense of original sin and guilt, Dr Price, fantastically garbed in a green and blue costume, chanted a 'Song of the Primitive Bard to the Moon'. He performed rites which he declared were druidic. A few disciples (he was never without them all his life) clustered around the authoritative doctor, who held a crescent-topped staff. Onlookers were sometimes inclined to mockery. Yet did those who were of the old true birth find their blood oddly stirred in racial memory? For this — so the local bards claimed — was the place of the Grey Cairns with their urns of bones, the place of dark pools where the ancient priests planted the water-lily whose stem symbolized the umbilical cord, and this was the monolith where the dim ecclesiastical poets gathered for worship of the goddess Cariadwen, Queen of Heaven and Mother of Gwen, the bardic Venus.

Newcomers might deride the doctor's queer flamboyance in this. But no one could mock at his growing fame as a very successful physician and surgeon. And the ill-paid miners could not complain of his habit of giving them his services free of charge; usually he extracted payment only from the rich. Also, he was known to assist, professionally, materially and spiritually, outcast girls condemned by the chapels — but in this what could be expected of a man who did not believe in the necessity of the legal marriage ceremony and, moreover, used to roam the mountains stark naked, declaring the sun a healing power? Despite his socialistic preachings, too, he had secured a firm friend in Francis Crawshay after he had been summoned to the ironmaster's castle and saved the life of Mrs Crawshay by performing a Caesarean operation. Following this, Dr Price and Crawshay would sometimes walk in a grove of oaks discoursing on druidic lore.

The poetic whisking-up of bygone mysticism was soon followed by something else. At a public meeting he announced: 'Man is greater than God, for man created God in his own image. The chapel preachers never lead the people except at funerals. They are always on the side of the rich and are merely concerned with seeing that the people believe in the divine origin of landlords and masters.' There were other pronouncements, infuriating to the strong hierarchy of chapel ministers and deacons, who began retaliating by spreading it about that the heathen Dr Price had disinterred the body of his father and cut off the head for some baleful rite. The body had certainly been exhumed, but only so that Dr Price could conduct a post-mortem to settle a law case in which it was claimed that his father had suffered from a mental disease.

That affair had led to the first of his many appearances in the courts. His second was in connexion with a claim to the Ruperra estate, which, he declared, had originally belonged to the druids and had been bequeathed to his father by its actual owner. In the 725 folios (now in the Public Record Office) which he deposited in support of this claim, he based his contention on the 'authority vested in the primitive bard to govern the world'. It was reported that, not surprisingly, 'nothing came of the matter'. But his appearances in court were always spectacular. He was allowed to give long eloquent speeches. Once he sued a bailiff for the sum of tenpence. Indicted for perjury at another time, and dressed in a smock of fine linen and a shawl of Royal Tartan plaid, he refused to be sworn on the Bible, and addressed the jury thus:

'As my brain has been ploughed and harrowed for the last five months, and sown by the conspirators with the seeds of villainy and malice, I beg you to listen to me patiently and with all the indulgence you can afford, while I, an innocent victim of persecution, mow down their harvest of perjury ....' Then later, 'Cannot her Majesty, as the Mighty Huntress, in her day, before the Lord, go out like the sun to find beasts of prey enough for her bloodhounds without hunting them to sacrifice the liberty and life of an innocent man upon her criminal alters with the bloody hands of her priesthood? What! Does the equivalent Queen of Great Britain, the mistress of the civilized world, in her day, fear the light of the sun living in a drop of dew and identified in the name of William Price?'

Were Victoria's jurymen flummoxed? Always conducting his own case, he showed, beyond the rhetoric, a legal knowledge that was greatly respected in the courts — knowledge which was to yield him great triumph in the *cause célèbre* that shed a fiery lustre on the last years of his life. Perhaps his denunciations of the law and lawyers were enjoyed in the courts. In one case he took with him to court his infant daughter Iarlles and constantly referred to her as his 'learned counsel'. Everybody looked forward to a Price law case.

In those ever-growing valleys pressed into dark slavery he established a fireside treasury of tales before he reached middle age. He strode about in his eccentrically brilliant garb, an early believer in this public-relations gambit, and he spread in dwellings and on the Common, and by a printed pamphlet or two, theories and opinions flatly contradictory to accepted notions. At the same time he often rescued a limb from amputation, cured a disease abandoned as hopeless by another doctor, and at one time performed a locally famous operation by grafting a piece of bone from a calf's leg on to a collier's limb crushed in the pit.

'This unscientific, money-making and superstitious profession!' he denounced his medical brethren. Declaring that doctors should pay the expenses of people they had allowed to fall ill, he added: 'We are suffering under the curse of the past mistakes of our profession. We have been educating the public into the false belief that poisonous drugs can give health. This belief has become such a deep-rooted superstition, that those of us who know better and who would like to adopt more rational methods, can only do so at the risk of losing our practice and reputation. The average doctor is at his best but a devoted bigot to this damnable teaching which we call medical art, and which alone in this age of science, has made no perceptible progress since the days of its earliest teachers. Some call it recognized science, but I call it recognized ignorance!' He never lost his contempt of medicine and pills, and all his life he spread a gospel of vegetarianism. Champagne was his sole table extravagance.

During the many strikes and agitations which even in those days were giving the valleys an added notoriety the doctor could not be expected to hold his tongue. To the coal lords he thundered, 'You are the Welsh Pharaohs who think you can suck the life-blood of the colliers for ever. You have grown fat and prosperous; you own the big houses; you wear the finest clothes; your children are healthy and happy; yet you do not work. How then have you got these things by idleness? Let me tell you. You have been stealing the balance of the low wages you have been paying them! Take heed, you men whose bodies and souls are bloated by the life-blood of the poor, take heed before it is too late. Remember that the oppression of the Pharaohs of Egypt did not last for ever, and neither will the oppression of the blood-sucking Pharaohs of Wales.' He was among the first of those who contributed a share towards making this race of workers so conscious of its power that later the South Wales area became one of the world's bravest battlefields for industrial reform. To the men, he said, 'There are two worlds. Not heaven and earth, but the world of the mansion and the world of the cottage, the world of the master and the world of the slave; the world of the exploiter and the world of the exploited; and between these two worlds there has begun a relentless and a grim struggle. And remember that there can never be peace in society until the world of the master and the exploiter is abolished. Then, and only then, will the toilers come into their own and all men shall enjoy the fruits of their labour.'

Such basic socialistic outbursts were delivered in 1839. Then Dr Price vanished from the haggard valleys for some time. After the Chartist rising of that year he was obliged to hide in Paris. He had long been a supporter of the Chartist movement and was a friend of John Frost, the Monmouthshire draper who, after the Newport insurrection, was sentenced to death for his part in it but, following national protest, found himself transported to Tasmania instead. On the rejection by Parliament of the Chartist petition it had been decided that in the ensuing rising a South Wales contingent should march on Newport and seize the town. Dr Price was appointed leader of the Pontypridd section. He gave a two-hour speech at a secret meeting of his armed men among the mountains, finishing: 'Let all cowards go their way, for they have no part to play in this great struggle. Men of the valleys, remember that the principle behind Chartism is the principle which acknowledges the right of every man who toils to the fruits of his labour. Every man here tonight must be unafraid to speak his mind, and unafraid to act according to his conscience, I am with you all the way — I, Doctor William Price.' The attack on Newport the next day was an abject failure; the authorities had gained knowledge of it, and in the historic battle outside the Westgate Hotel many Chartists were killed by a detachment of soldiers.

A warrant out for his arrest, and the ports of the Bristol Channel watched, Dr Price went to ground for a day or two — and then had the satisfaction of being helped to board a ship at Cardiff by Police Inspector Stockdale, who was on quayside duty with warrants for Price and others in his pocket. The person the inspector so kindly assisted up the ship's gangway was an unaccompanied lady who appeared to be a little unwell at the prospect of a rough voyage. Dr Price had sacrificed his fine beard.

In Paris he was befriended by a rich compatriot, Captain Phelps, became acquainted with Heine, another exile, and practised as a doctor. But druidism was not forgotten. In the Louvre he excitedly discovered a precious stone inscribed with mysterious hieroglyphs which he alone of all mankind could decipher. Twenty centuries ago, he announced, it had been ordained that this 'Druid's stone' would be discovered by himself and thereby convey to him regal power and the authority of the old religion; the hieroglyphs had yielded their secret to him. This agile intellectual exercise achieved, he next involved himself in a scandal and a quarrel with his Welsh benefactor. Captain Phelps had found that his daughter's absences from home were not always spent with the tutoring Dr Price in the Louvre. The doctor had been teaching the principles of sun-worship to the beautiful sixteen-year-old girl, and the naked couple were discovered gambolling and caressing in a bosky retreat outside the city.

He stayed in Paris until it was safe for him to return to Wales. Pontypridd, except for his watchful chapel enemies there, was glad to see him back, and it was not long before he was engaged in a new series of litigations, mostly over property and his desire to build a 'palace' for himself near the traditional burial-place of druids in the town. He began work — illegally — on this building, and was ejected by feudal Lady Llanover, who still kept a bardic harpist on her domestic staff. But he had managed to erect two towers (still in existence in 1968) which were to serve as an imposing gateway to the domain and, besieged in one of these round, fortress-like structures, with creditors on the prowl, his two daughters nailed him into a chest and carried it safely out. Once more he escaped arrest and went into hiding.

The women in his life remained (except for the final one) anonymous. It is his children, often seen with him in the Pontypridd streets, who are recalled in memories. 'I have found it unnecessary to enter into any legal marriage,' the father announced, 'because I do not, as an evolved being, require any law or religious ceremony to compel me to love the woman I have chosen as my mate. The artificial thunder of the Church and the State on marriage cannot frighten me to live with any woman under compulsion. No law made by God or man can compel a man or a woman to love each other, but it can and does compel them to live with each other, which is quite another matter.' He believed that lovers should enter in a probationary period of union, and that a marriage should be freely dissolved by mutual consent, the community only intervening to safeguard 'that which is of vital interest to it, the children'.

With his dominant character, presence, romantic costumes and theories, he did not seem to have been obliged to bludgeon a woman and bear her off to druidic lairs in the mountains. According to gossip, there were many women in his long life; if it was true, they kept obscurely to their unknown hearths, perhaps contentedly. But eventually he settled at Llantrisant village, four or five miles beyond Pontypridd, accompanied by the woman who was the last of his loves, Gwenllian Llewyllyn. They occupied a cottage called Ty'r Clettwr and had with them their two children. Depicted in an engraving of the time, Gwenllian was remarkably handsome, a calm madonna sitting with a naked child on her knees.

In this medieval village Dr Price spent the rest of his life and, towards its close, achieved his last grand flouting of seemly custom. Meanwhile, in addition to receiving patients from all over Wales, he pursued his druidic studies, wrote memoirs, and spread his gospels of industrial reform. His extreme difference from the local miners' leader and M.P., Mabon, and the later Keir Hardie and John Burns, was not only that he harangued the men wearing his arresting costume, but in his everyday life brought a dash of wild poetry to the valleys. The bee in his fox-skin bonnet hummed from a need to give people liberty beyond the prosaic advantages of better wages and pit conditions. He did not lose faith in the old druidic gods. Such gods alone had respect for sacred bards and their riddles which were linked to the principles of life. He wanted the old race back, with its bright-striped coats and purple cloaks, its lime-washed dyed hair and its circumspect hospitality to strangers at the gate.

He did not lose belief in one of the other reputed customs of pagans either, and at last the police were able to nab him for this. Far younger than himself, Gwenllian Llewyllyn bore him a son at Llantrisant. Dr Price was then eighty-one. The boy was named Iesu Grist. His Merlin father, who seemed able to trace some relation between druidism and the Saviour, announced that this most loved child would restore the full splendour of the druidic kingdom to the world. The boy died in early infancy.

Among Dr Price's hygienic, vegetarian, anti-chapel and other preachings he had always advocated cremation and had already burned dead animals. But no one was prepared for the dreadful act he now perpetrated in a walled field he owned above the village at the very time when the Llantrisant chapel was conducting a Christian service below. The act roused to full fury the latent hostility he had earned in the past from most of the locality. It was also to bring him wide fame, in addition to posthumous canonization by the Cremation Society of Great Britain. The date was 13 January 1884. The father carried his son's body, wrapped in linen, to the field called Caerlan. A cask of paraffin waited there. Dr Price lit a wide ring of fire about this altar, placed the body on the cask, and set a torch to the oil. He remained chanting within the circle of fire. But news of his blasphemous intention had quickly spread and men were assembling; by the time the chapel had emptied others were speeding up to the field, some armed with sticks and cudgels. The police had also been informed. Two constables hurried up, arriving in time to prevent the unmoved doctor from being assaulted, if not lynched; they drew their batons. One constable, cape over head, dashed to the cask and snatched out the half-burned body.

Dr Price was taken into custody and conveyed to Pontypridd police station — for his own safety, the police later contended. The whole district was set by the ears. But the doctor, released after one night's detention, remained unruffled. At an inquest on the body the coroner found himself unable to grant permission to the police to bury it. Dr Price was claiming ownership, and also refusing not to attempt cremation again — 'I am not asking you to return to me the body of my child,' he said. 'I am demanding it.' The body was returned to him. Ignoring the dangerous hostility he had roused, and denounced from pulpits all over Wales, he carried the cremation through some weeks later at the same spot. He was not molested. It was known that a legal prosecution of him was being instituted. But that night a mob attacked his cottage with stones. Shouting figures called on the old heretic to come out and face them. Suddenly the door opened and Gwenllian Llewyllyn appeared, a pistol in each hand. She threatened to shoot. The mob dispersed.

Price was indicted at the next Cardiff assizes, for cremating the dead body of a child. Dressed in a snowy linen robe and a coloured shawl, he spoke in court with his usual eloquence and legal knowledge. The case became famous throughout the world. Mr Justice Stephen ruled that cremation of the dead was not illegal provided that it was carried out in such a manner as not to constitute a public nuisance at common law. After his acquittal, Price instituted proceedings against the Pontypridd police for false imprisonment and was awarded damages. He also caused a commemoration medal of the cremation to be struck, and sold thousands of these at threepence each. Shoals of letters arrived at Ty'r Clettwr in praise of the epic act on Caerlan Field. For the first time in Christian Britain cremation had received legal sanction, and within a year practice of it began in a crematorium at Woking.

The aged gadfly did not rest. He became active in a project to build an ornate crematorium for Wales. It came to nothing; profit from the medals was not enough and response to an appeal for funds was poor. There were a few years of quiet. Local hostility became mingled with a grudging realization that a great if peculiar man was resident at Llantrisant. Patients still flocked to him from far and near and still he did not expect payment from those too poor for it. Then, in 1890, there was an event which could not but rouse universal respect and admiration. At the age of eighty-seven, the vegetarian and champagne-drinker once more — and for the last time — became a father. This boy also was named Iesu Grist (and, surviving for long at Llantrisant, was cremated in the everyday manner in 1960). His father lived for three years more, receiving patients up to a week before his death. It was reported that he drank a final glass of champagne just before going to join his druid brethren of the antique past.

He had not done with earthly magnificence. Detailed instructions had been left for the disposal of his body, including 'No sorrowing and no black clothes'. His memorial was to be a painted sixty-foot pole crowned with a crescent moon. He had already designed and supervised the construction of his iron coffin at a Llantrisant blacksmith's forge, and such instructions as the amount of coal to be used and the manner of lighting the pyre were explicit. All his wishes were observed by Gwenllian Llewyllyn and his faithful band of disciples, and the doctor himself would not have been offended by the vast crowds of spectators that assembled, together with dozens of his old enemies, the police, on the morning of 31 January 1893. People had begun trekking from the valleys long before dawn.

Attired in his brightly coloured clothes and fox-skin head-dress, he lay in the muslin-draped coffin. It was carried out of Ty'r Clettwr on a bier and borne up to Caerlan Field, followed by Gwenllian, the gaily-clad Price children, and a few friends. Hundreds of admission tickets to the field had been issued. The police were needed; the many thousands of people without tickets pressed up the slope in excited fascination. In the field a hasty structure of masonry, packed with shavings, wood and paraffin-soaked coal, had been built. It contained an open oven. Three tons of coal and one of wood lay near by.

Policemen were forced to help the bearers carry the iron coffin up the slope and place it in the pioneering crematorium. Two friends of the doctor's applied torches. After witnessing the first flames curling about the coffin the family returned to Ty'r Clettwr. Stokers remained to feed a rapidly mounting fire. The coffin lay in the oven for eight hours; it became red hot and flames could be seen issuing from the holes Dr Price had designed in its sides. It was withdrawn with long iron hooks and found to be shattered. When cool, what remained inside was carried back, escorted by police, to Ty'r Clettwr. The crowds had broken into the field. Earlier, they had to be beaten back by the police so that the stokers could do their work.

He remained alive in anecdotes for long. An illustrated memorial sheet of his cremation was printed. The tall pole with its crescent moon was remembered by many people who were too young to understand its significance; that it cracked and fell in a great storm seemed a fitting link with the old rebel's adventures. The Cremation Society erected a tablet at Llantrisant to commemorate the legal sanction of Dr Price's daring performance on Caerlan Field. But in the hoary village and elsewhere in Wales harsh criticism of his character persisted for long. A daughter, Penelope, survives in breezy Llantrisant (1968) and, understandably, keeps the reputation of her illustrious father shining bright as a lamp.

Dr Price dropped good seed. He kept a sharp eye on the arrival of the Industrial Revolution in Wales. With his exceptional talents as a doctor he could have earned position and fortune in some more luxurious place than those valleys filled with an oppressed people whose 'degraded condition', a Royal Commissioner reported in 1847, 'I regard as entirely the fault of their employers, who give them far less tendance and care than they bestow on their cattle.' But he chose to stay among his people and, throughout his life, to lift to his lips an old battle-horn. He was a descendant of the warrior-bards who were always at the side of those Welsh kings and leaders incensed by the attempts of invaders to obliterate the ancient heritage of their race. Instead of foreign soldiers he had coal owners and iron-masters to grapple with — more subtle invaders. His task was to ensure that they should not utterly possess the spirit of his people.

His many speeches to the miners and iron-workers were devoid of the mystic poetry that convoluted his druidic utterances; they were shrewd, full of common sense, contained an ability to perceive the future, and they glowed. But that was not all. He was a member of a race that is moonstruck, that has never quite forgotten the primitive magic of natural forces, that loves unbridled songs and rhythms and drama. Before the Reformation members of the true race had danced and told their flower-tinted tales in an imaginative awareness of the sensuous world. Later there was the Nonconformist blight, which nevertheless in its first vigour canalized the old poetry into displays of magnificent oratory and into lyrical hymns, only to become a grey obliterating nineteenth-century cloud frowning over a confused people. Dr Price saw this and endeavoured to invoke the moon's magical touch again. He saw that a fatter wage-packet was not enough.

'All very well for him,' I heard my mother say on one occasion, as she recalled her Pontypridd glimpses of the wicked old eccentric and flouter of the wedding ceremony. 'He enjoyed showing-off and people talking and staring. But what about his poor children going through life illegitimate? And calling them names like Iesu Grist and Countess of Glamorgan! All that nonsense about druids too! The druids can't come back — not with coalmines here and a man like D.A. Thomas in charge of us.'

Four: Children's Games

After the noisy turbulence of Saturday nights the constitution of Sunday, with all pubs locked into silence, belonged almost entirely to our sermon-and-choir-loving God. Only singing from the chapels was to be heard in Clydach Vale streets. The Cambrian pit-hooter did not blow except late in the evening, calling grown men to the night-shift. The hoarse, weather-beaten Crier did not shake his tarnished bell at important street corners and announce a forthcoming Miners' Federation meeting addressed by Mabon, or a concert, the visit of a circus or menagerie to Pandy Field, a stoppage of water supply during pipe repairs, a cheap excursion to Porthcawl or Barry Island by special train from Tonypandy, and once, I remember, the death of a king, Edward VII. A peculiar bereftness haunted the streets on Sundays. It made me morose.

Sitting flannel-shirted in Gosen chapel, the expert choir-singing crashed disregarded over my head; such heavenly noises were not a taste of mine, perhaps because I couldn't sing a note. But Mr Walters's sermons never failed to plant guilt with a firm hand, and after its impregnation a necessity for redemption was with me, if only intermittently. The preacher's denunciations and warnings were conveyed to me mostly by his facial contortions and tonal management of thundering; brooding boys couldn't be expected to cope with the verbal intricacies of Welsh *hwyl*. But the grey messages penetrated deep beyond my itching skin. My sins weighed on me much more than the logical expectation of punishment for them following discovery. There was the theft of half a sovereign from our shop, with which I bought a box of watercolours in Tonypandy, hiding it in my school desk; after the showdown I was only half punished by a brisk thrashing from my father with a cane specially bought in Perkins's ironmongery shop three doors up.

Enjoyment of sins never could be perfect. One of them, however, eluded discovery, punishment and seizure by claws, and

I pondered on its core of pleasure for long with satisfaction. I married when I was twelve. The union was brief, its ceremony and crowning act enacted in a coke oven, and the parting of husband and wife immediate.

The disused coke ovens, used in bygone days for carbonization of inferior coal, had belonged to a small, pioneering mine sloping down into the mountain-side across the bridged river. Ten of them, they ranged along a grassy bank, iron doors still hanging loose on several of the beehive-like structures. Old strips of corrugated zinc covered the holes in the arched brick roofs of those which were used now for keeping pigs and chickens in. A billy goat lived in one. In the one next to it card-playing gamblers foregathered on their atheistic Sundays; they kept wooden boxes there for seats and a table, and the rusty door hid the sinners from sight. I married Vanna in this one.

She was a dark girl of exotic Italy, with a mushroom-pale skin, her face eager as the black mane of strong curls running down to her shoulders. Born among us, like her brother Aldo, her parents had come childless from North Italy to Clydach Vale in its genesis days. Young colliers congregated in their pop, ice-cream and sweets shop, which had benches and penny-in-the-slot machines. Aldo, with whom I was friendly, sometimes gave me a free ice-cream cornet from the painted handcart he plied in the streets on Saturdays. His father was cruel and beat him regularly in their backyard, where the ice-cream was churned every day and scraggy fowls looked frightened. Yet, always smiling, Aldo remained gay as his pink, blue and white cart, an example of triumphant manhood arrived at early fruit. He piled ice-cream extravagantly high in the halfpenny cornets, perhaps to spite his mean father. I much admired Aldo and, in the Italian way, he admired my admiration. His sister, about three years younger than him, must have been rising thirteen when I married her.

Idwal, an outwards-looking friend of mine at that time, married us. A leader in our school class, he always treated Vanna with the disinterested contempt of the 100 per cent extrovert; she was a tomboy, often joined in our street games, seemed to have no girlfriends but owned a skipping rope with wooden handles and, her mane whirling, could skip a couple of hundred jumps without stopping. No doors opened into Idwal's granite heart for her or anyone else. He possessed natural authority, a finely soaring soprano voice and a talent for accurate mimicry of grown men and women. He wore a surplice in St Thomas's church choir, and for the event in the coke oven on a quiet August holiday afternoon he smuggled this out of his home, where his mother had given it its monthly washing and starching. Garbed in it, he fixed rimless pince-nez on the tip of his nose. Four boxes formed an altar. On it stood a bottle of ginger pop Vanna had stolen from her parents' shop, a Church of England prayer book and a Christmas cracker ring which had a blue stone.

Vanna spread a lacy handkerchief over her hair. Idwal, standing before the altar, stopped her giggles with a forbidding squint above the pince-nez. It should have been a warning to me of their confederacy. I was not really a school dunce or entirely retarded, but I was not as bright as Idwal, though my eyes saw more than his. Opening the prayer book, he looked serious as a funeral and his soprano took on a deep underswell. He did not intone all the marriage service, and since I did not know the ceremony then, I could not suspect that this scampering had a motive.

'You put the ring on her finger now, boy *bach*,' he censured me. 'Pay attention.'

The ring on, he blessed us from the prayer book, took a first long swig from the bottle and passed it to us. 'I'll keep guard outside the door,' he promised, pulling his surplice off and removing his pince-nez. 'If it's two whistles there's someone coming.' Vanna's short neck swelled thick as she swallowed a bride's mouthful of pop, then passed the bottle to me. Outside, Idwal gave the iron door a shove, closing it as far as it could go on its broken hinges. Sufficient light came from a chink there, and from under the loose zinc sheet covering the hole in the roof, for me to see a gleam in Vanna's dancing eye. Looking round at me, she put a knee on the altar. She lay full length on it and whipped up the front of her frock. She wore no drawers. I saw the forbidden mystery. It was like a dusky apricot.

There was an ugly clatter. A shaft of hard daylight flooded the oven. The sheet of corrugated zinc had been hurled aside. A face lay over the edge of the hole. 'Hey, what d'you think you're doing down there?' The guttural voice cracked. 'Sergeant Richards here!' The face vanished. 'Get the handcuffs on him, Jenkins.' I had tumbled on to the ground. Vanna's squeal as she had leapt up was as unnerving. She pushed the door half open and ran. By the time I scrambled up and got outside she had rounded the row of ovens. Idwal, hands on hips, stood grinning cynically, on the bank above. 'No good chasing her, *boy bach*. Legs like a whippet's.' He leapt down. 'Better than a game of marbles, eh?'

Yet I did not feel I had been fooled; I even felt well-disposed towards Idwal, although somewhere inside myself I also began to reject him. That same week, as if I had provided *him* with pleasure, he gave me a bull's-eye marble, and, to my surprise, he did not gab about the coke oven event to schoolfriends. Vanna's conduct became as strange. She ignored me after our marriage. I vainly sought opportunity to speak to her. When we passed in the main street, almost every day, her gaze became fixed on her lifted nose. Even more surprisingly, she did not join us again in our back-lane games — she used to play marbles with us, squatting beside the marked ring like a boy. A Catholic, she attended a tin church in Tonypandy which had been built for the poor Irish immigrants who sought a less hard life in the Rhondda. I had heard that Catholics rid themselves of anything nasty by kneeling before a priest in a cupboard. Had Vanna confessed her marriage and been forbidden to associate with me? A few months after the marriage she put her hair up, much earlier in life than was the practice of Welsh girls. Then suddenly I saw her no more in the street.

'Where's Vanna gone?' I asked my brother-in-law one day, across the handcart. I felt I had a right to ask.

'Italy.' Aldo's smile at me, because it was perpetual, had no significance. But he had given me a quick glance. 'Turin. With our grandmother. Not coming back.' Licking my cornet, I lingered in dissatisfaction. He took up the cart-handles and trundled off without another word to me.

Time eased my sense of bondage and deprivation. Three or four years later the whole family vanished as abruptly as Vanna had. It was said that they had made a small fortune, pit strikes and lock-outs notwithstanding. Before the marriage I had been permitted once into their living-room behind the shop. Its peasant starkness astonished me; nothing covered the wood planks of the floor, there were no ornaments, no fender before the ash-filled grate. The savage father, weighing an ounce of chocolate dragees in the shop, would break one in half for exact balance on the scales. But the mother, who had an intimidating line of moustache on her lip, gave overweight; those boys who knew of her foolishness would wait until she appeared behind a counter heaped with a variety of sweets unobtainable in other shops. Like her son, she always smiled at us.

Idwal, only a few weeks after the event in the coke oven, victimized me once more, though this time he could not really be blamed. His plan went awry through no fault of his, and I was the main culprit, though in my case too I hadn't counted on an incalculable power taking charge, sudden as one of our fierce mountain showers of rain.

Mrs Blow had a pear tree. The only flourishing pear tree in the place, it was a big, well-known tree soaring above the back garden wall of Mrs Blow's end house in a quiet side street leading down to the river. When it blossomed people took walks down there to view this authentic confirmation of spring's arrival. There were a few scraggy apple trees in other gardens, and a plum or two, but none like Mrs Blow's pear tree. Nobody knew why it bore fruit so richly for her, why it grew to such a size, why it was there at all, making a country orchard of her grey corner.

She was bad-tempered, a goitered widow living alone, bulky in all her parts. Her collier husband had died years before; something had happened to him down-under, and she lived on 'compo' money from the Cambrian company and the brewing of her nettle beer, penny a bottle and the best in the place. If she was in a temper she would refuse to sell bottles to persons she didn't like, often abusing them on her doorstep. On winter days of high wind or driving rain she had a habit of walking backwards up to the main road shops — there was a turning that caught the full rage of our gales — because, she said, wind made her tender eyes water like roof-spouts. But her heroic posterior slowly advancing up the slope brought a sense of ominous power about to exact full reckoning with her many critics. She was an occasional non-credit customer in my father's shop.

'Meet me tonight at ten outside Noddfa Chapel,' Idwal ordained. 'They're ripe. She goes to bed early.' It was early September and we had returned to school.

I skulked out past our stable into the back lane and collected Idwal. We had string bags in our pockets. Mrs Blow's corner house lay in darkness; we pushed back the letter-flap of her door and peered in. Nobody was to be seen in this last street down by the railway's incline for coaltrucks. Across the corner, a gas street-lamp dimly picked out fruits hanging far above Mrs Blow's back wall. Idwal was well aware of my advantages for the raid. I had a jockey lightness of body, a cat's sureness of foot, and I had won a silver medal for a sprinting event in our school sports. Thickset and squat, Idwal was clumsy. He came up the wall with the aid of my hand from above.

'Go to the top,' he whispered. 'Best ones on top. There's some down here for me. I can stretch.' He stood on the wall, gripping a low branch. I swung up into the big tree with ease. Golden flasks hung plump among the arms of leaves. 'Go on,' Idwal urged. 'Higher.' But, straddling a swaying fork of branches, my back against the trunk, I could go no farther. I took out my string bag. My hand closed round a cool little belly, and the fleshy shape, free-of-charge for its plucking, excited me. Then the branches quaked and creaked. The whole tree shook.

I saw a swinging lantern below. But it was Idwal who had warningly shaken the branches. Then he was gone; I heard the scrape of his boots running on the road an instant before Mrs Blow's voice shot up from her garden. 'Thief, thief! Police, police!' Flickers of light penetrated the tree. I could see a candle in the cart-lamp she held aloft. 'Come down, you!' Her terrible voice rose higher. 'Police! Got you this time! Down you come, you thief!'

Ague trapped me tighter in the fork. My knees trembled, yet could not move into action. Simultaneously came an agonized need to water. About to do it in my knickerbockers, as often happened to sickly Willie Morgans in school, I managed to unbutton, let loose, and, peeing into the thick net of leaves below, even then thought of our horse stopping before the field of dandelions flashed through my mind. The sweet physical relief vanished. Mrs Blow's cries rose to a bellow. 'Ah, you dirty ruffian! Police, police! Dirty pig! ... Mrs Howells ....

She was summoning her neighbour for witness. It galvanized me. I reached the top of the wall with monkey certainty. The lantern shone up on me for a second. 'I know you! Dirty pig ....' I jumped. Still there was nobody to be seen on the road. I ran towards the main street, and saw Idwal. Eating a pear, he stood peering round the entrance to a back lane a few yards up the slope. 'I heard her shouting,' he said, following me as I dashed into the darkness. 'She's bluffing. Everybody steals her pears.'

I did not tell him of my shameful lapse. He gave me the half-eaten pear, our only loot. It was a hard one, but my mouth was dry. I couldn't believe Mrs Blow had been able to recognize me in the lantern's faint light. She hadn't called my name. But thought of the police cells in the station up the main road haunted me. Mrs Blow kept a school slate in her front parlour window, *Pears 4d. a bag* chalked on it. So our game was like stealing in a shop. Idwal brushed my dread aside. He said she must have sat at her back window expecting everybody to go up her tree.

By the time I returned from school the following afternoon the panic was forgotten. My mother followed me into our living-room from the empty shop. Esther, our servant and my close friend, gave me one of her underlid looks. She took the cosy off the teapot as usual, then put it back. Before I could sit at the table my mother pointed at the black leather sofa. 'Sit there,' she said. 'Mrs Blow came in this afternoon.' Even she looked withdrawn from me. 'What made you do it?' She took a closing-in position before the sofa. I knew her implacable look; she sometimes had it for rapscallion customers in the shop.

'I didn't steal any pears,' I shouted. 'I only climbed the tree with Idwal. He bet me I couldn't go to the top.'

'He bet you? You know very well what I mean. You did something else. Why did you do it?'

It dawned on me that the other thing had been put into words. By women! Thieving was nothing in comparison. I hung my head. 'She frightened me,' I whimpered. 'Screaming at me at the top of her voice. I couldn't help it.'

There was a long, slow scrutiny of me. 'Give him his tea,' she said impatiently to Esther, and returned to the shop. My father had gone to Cardiff on business. Esther kept silent for a minute, then said, 'Your mother gave her a tablecloth and half a pound of best tea.' There were always two or three of these linen tablecloths in our chest of drawers; one would be presented to any daughter of good customers on marriage.

'Everybody steals her pears,' I hedged, wondering how much Esther knew. She too seemed an enemy then, ranged with other women on their side of a fence.

'Well, it wasn't the pears, was it? Mrs Blow came in here to tell your mother. Wouldn't say it in the shop. Drenched, she said she was.'

This extravagance was too much for me. Mrs Blow was so big that a bucketful would have been needed. 'It went on the leaves,' I protested. 'Hundreds of them under me.'

'Leaves shake,' the country girl pointed out. 'You had to get out of the tree, didn't you?'

'Why didn't she move from under it, then?'

'It was her tree.' Esther had an obstinate look. 'No business you had to be up it.' This was the first time she had displayed censure of me since she had come to us two years before.

No punishment was meted out by my mother or father. My fear had been enough, its outcome a natural act of God beyond the jurisdiction of police or family powers. As far as I knew, the affair was hushed up. But, like other guilts, it weighed on me for long. I avoided going to where the pear tree grew; I scampered if I saw the widow's unmistakable bulk afar in the main road or, on bad winter days, backing towards its corner like a ship coming slowly into harbour. To me she was no longer a target for mocking humour.

She died two or three years later. Her freckled goitre was the most obdurate in the place, where examples of that valley affliction were many. It was not until she had gone, and I overheard some talk in our shop, that I learned that her collier husband had died from 'silicosis', as everybody called the pneumoconiosis which was one of the many curses of work below the valley's floor. He had been buried from a Home, away over the mountains, where bad sufferers went for cure or no cure. That was why, despite her wicked temper which had kept general esteem of her at bay, she was given a grand funeral. It was not usual for members of colliers' lodges to turn out with their panoply of great silken banners for the funeral of a woman. They had been unable to do this for Mrs Blow's husband. So she was proxy for it.

I went to view her funeral's rise from outside her house, in the Whitsun school holiday, when her pear tree was in full blossom. It eased my guilt to see such a ceremonious send-off. There were shining black horses, a glass hearse instead of the hand-bier which often was all the poor could afford, and, as was customary, the crowd of men sang a hymn outside the house. The embroidered banners, each with two poles and four tasselled golden ropes held fore and aft by lodge members, billowed in a breeze as the procession wound up to the main road. There would be singing

44

for most of the two miles to the capacious cemetery down in Trealaw, a domain unknown to me then. My small presence among the pack of onlookers, most of them grown-ups, was all I could offer. I was glad Idwal was not there.

Five: Esther

She was a true country girl. Anyone arriving in the Rhondda from the standstill rustic parts needed to wear a different pair of life's boots with us, and for a long time Esther pretended to be comfortable in hers. Except for a good sprinkling of Irish and Bristol-way invaders, nearly everybody of full stature had hailed from the Welsh arcadies, or their parents had, and most newcomers soon felt at home and ceased to sigh for the lost innocences of country places. Esther continued to talk of her native shire. Sometimes they had fierce seas there, but the weather was quite different in that clement spot which bordered the Atlantic, a patch or two of yellow corn waving in gentle pulsations under ever-blue skies, peaceful cattle keeping want unfailingly at bay for the lucky owners. Once or twice, however, she referred to the bad poverty that had brought her to us, for thirty shillings a month and her keep. Yet, after almost four years, she was to lose heart and return to the scenes she had left, though not before she struck her own private blow for our angry place.

Her cheeks were fuschia-red, and her sorrel hair filled an enamel bowl when she washed it every Wednesday, her half-day off. I first saw her as she was laying the tea-table in our living-room when I arrived from the elementary school just above Dai Morgan's slaughter-house on the mountain's lower slope. I was about nine then. Esther couldn't have been more than nineteen. Her brother had come to Clydach Vale to work in D.A. Thomas's Cambrian pit months before; he lodged with one of my father's customers and had sought a place for his sister. Esther arrived with a roped tin trunk and a 'transfer' letter from the minister of her Baptist chapel in Cardigan to a fellow minister in Clydach Vale. She had enough English words for the conveyance of such thoughts as she wished to disclose, and very soon — my own tutoring was of aid — picked up the more or less alien tongue profusely.

For some weeks she had refused to go out. On her afternoon off she would sit at one of the two windows of our front room upstairs and stare down at the main road as if foreseeing dire things happening there. The big Central pub opposite, open all day, especially held her attention. Her brother, who was not as good-looking as she, came to see her sometimes in a criss-crossed muffler and a cap, already a young collier well in with the boyos and not one to shun the Central; he would wink at me from the sofa as if we both must have patience with women. Of course I had quickly sensed Esther's inferior position and taken advantage of it in demands for services and attentions. She was not of truculent character, and we rapidly established amicable relations. Her habit of modestly keeping her eyelids down pleased me. In return for her stories of country life I educated her in arithmetic, English spelling and other simplicities during my school home- work at our large table, while she ironed at one end. Lessons in her own school had been conducted in Welsh and she seemed to want to reapprehend even arithmetic through the English language.

Only a few months after her arrival there came an incident that, although it was not truly an example of my Little Master arro- gance, was to bring me acute embarrassment years later. My grandparents paid an unexpected visit from Ynysybwl, stayed the night, and, since we had only three bedrooms, I was put to sleep with Esther in her small back room. Unaccustomed to sharing a bed with anyone, I did not sleep for a long time. Hard-working Esther went into slumber with a healthy lack of worry. Flat on her back, she lay breathing unfussily as a locomotive taking rest. The depths of night must have been reached when I put a hand up her nightdress. I received an eerie shock. I had touched an electrically tingling bush. It was like putting my fingers in a prickly nest still warm from a thrush's sitting. Esther gave a grunt and heaved over on to her side. Her back was an enormous negative which of course I accepted. Curiosity had been satisfied. I had not at that time married Vanna in the coke oven.

A boy's days are too full for excessive meditation on such a matter, and, besides, Esther must have been fast asleep. She had for me the grave respect which is of prime importance in fondness. She admired my learning when I sat with my homework copy- books; and she did not cackle or tease. A blemish in her was that she did not understand my horror of flannel shirts; in Cardigan, men and women were born into flannel and lived and died in it. She also admired my mother and imitated her in many respects, particularly in turns of speech. The two had a mania for washing their faces. It was a thorough ritual, bare arms whirling, our soft mountain water shooting out of the bowl, the drying done in sighing satisfaction. Both had wonderful skins. My mother, however, when she went to shop in Cardiff (though not when she went to chapel), tore a leaf or two out of a scented booklet called *Papier Pouire* and rubbed them briskly along her nose.

Esther liked best her quiet ironing sessions at evening. My mother would bustle in and out from the shop, seldom staying long, or be off for a talking hour with the knowledgeable midwife who lived near; my father, as soon as the shop closed, sped to his haunts — the Chamber of Trade premises in Tonypandy, football committee meetings, the Central, the new golf links club up on Pen Rhys mountain above Llwynypia. Esther would then settle. The exactitude of her folded sheets, tablecloths, towels, underwear and shirts had a geometric perfection as she draped them on the brass mantel-rod above our fireplace. The things had been washed by Mrs Gronw, wife of a heavy-drinking collier who took in tradespeople's washing, and they smelt faintly of the long bars of soap called Sensation.

Esther's pair of irons stood on a contraption fixed to the grate in which, summer and winter, the best Cambrian steam coal sparkled; we did not buy the tip-combings, costing a few pence, which a black-smudged woman gathered and carried through the back lanes in a sack on her shoulders. A testing gob of Esther's silver spit would hiss off an iron. Sometimes she sat on the scroll-end black sofa for a minute and looked mournfully far away from the clock-ticking room — another forewarning of distress to come, had I known it. Disliking heat, I sat with my copybooks at the table's end farthest away from the fireplace.

'In Cardigan they dip a chapel preacher into the sea when it's too rough to go out fishing,' she told me, on an evening of howling wind and rain. She shook her head when I asked her if she had seen this done; she had only heard of the placatory act, and that the preachers were always willing because it kept people religious. But she *had* known a village girl who had accidentally swallowed a tadpole in a mug of water and, weeks afterwards, began to 'swell up'. This arrested my attention.

'Her mother took her to an old witch we had, called Olwen,' Esther proceeded, carefully folding a starched linen tablecloth;

'and then the swelling went down in a jiffy.' I waited, knowing from Esther's face that more was to come. 'Died when she was nearly eighty.'

'You said it was a girl you knew,' I pointed out.

'Olwen the witch, I mean.' Esther's tone became more dramatic, suiting the history she related. 'Blockage it was, I heard.' I let this unknown term pass; death was death. 'Lived on the parish old-age pension with her sister Megan and a big cat away down a wood. Pigs and chickens outside their cottage, Megan clean as the white of day, but not Olwen the witch.' Esther shook out a pair of lace-edged cotton drawers. 'Well, the night before Olwen was going to be buried she got out of her coffin upstairs and called down to her sister, wanting something to eat.' I stopped twirling my pen and stared. Was Esther making fun of me? It would be the first time.

'She was dead,' I reminded her.

'Gone into a trance because of the blockage and stiff as a poker!' Esther cried triumphantly. 'Old Doctor Hopkins had signed 'stificate, and a man went there afterwards from the Teify paper that comes out on Fridays.' She shook a finger at me. 'Let me finish! Twelve o'clock at night it was when Megan heard her calling for food — she was downstairs late, baking a ham for the funeral next day, and she ran out screaming into the wood and stayed under a tree till her senses came back. Their cat started mewing and jumping like mad when Olwen called out for food, Megan said afterwards to Mrs James Post Office.' Esther spat on a reheated iron, and I had begun to believe the story. 'Well, Megan sat under the tree and thought she hadn't heard Olwen at all, late at night and worn out cooking and cleaning for the funeral. Back she went to the cottage. And there was the one that was dead frying a slice of bacon off the lump they always kept hanging! She never spoke, Megan said, but was glaring. Then Olwen took an egg from a basin of them on the dresser, fresh eggs from the hens they had, and she broke it into the frying-pan.' Esther ironed at her normal slow pace. 'It turned stinking black at once! She lifted it out and broke another egg. Black and stinking like the other one! Megan said the stink stinked all the house.' Esther turned the garment.

'*Stunk* the house,' I corrected, uncertain again.

Too absorbed in her recital to notice, Esther went on, 'Not a day old those eggs were! Megan couldn't stand it any more. She ran out again, she ran through the wood all the way to our village. Everybody safe in bed! She woke Mrs Pugh Ty Bach first, then Mrs Pugh woke Mrs Shinkins, then Mrs Whinkins woke us — "Olwen's risen up in her coffin and is frying *cig moch*," she shouted; "there'll have to be a man to go there." All the village came out of bed.' Esther looked at me, as if sensing my renewed doubt, but continued firmly, 'Not a man would go to the cottage — no indeed! Women's business it was, they said.... Listening are you?'

'Stop now,' I attempted to curb her. 'It's the eggs. Why were they stinking black, fresh from the chickens?'

'A witch Olwen was!' Esther insisted. 'I *told* you. And the men wouldn't go to the cottage because of that. They made excuse that Megan had dreamt it all and they went back to bed.' She changed irons, and shook out a blouse.

I had never known her to tell a lie; subterfuge had no place in her honest face, that she kept so clean. 'What happened then?' I asked, setting her outlandish explanation of the stinking black eggs aside.

'Well, Mrs James Post Office and Mrs Pugh Ty Bach went back with Megan. And there was Olwen sitting in a chair drinking her second cup of tea and a shawl over the white nightgown she wore in the coffin. "Weak I am," she said, "but nothing like I was before." Sight of Megan made her fly into a temper. "She's an old stoopid," she shouted top of her voice.' Esther glanced at me from under her lowered lids. 'A lot of awful words came from her. Mrs Pugh Ty Bach said to us afterwards a stink of bad eggs *was* in the cottage. She made remark about it to Olwen and the witch said Megan kept eggs in the basin for two or three months like heathens in Australia. But Megan said, no, the eggs were fresh, collected ready for anyone wanting them boiled in water after the funeral next day.'

'Did they send the coffin back?' I asked, still reserving my doubts.

'No. The old witch said she'd see her sister into it, and she kept it under the bed for blankets. She told the man from the Teify paper the same thing and she'd have money from the doctor, but the man didn't put that in his paper. All in Welsh it was in the paper and I saw it with my own pair of eyes. So there!' Her note of challenge rang true. 'There's nice tussore silk in this blouse!' She held up my mother's ironed garment admiringly, and finished, 'Olwen spoke right. Megan went three years before her. Seventy-seven she was. All she had new was a brass plate changed on the lid, that had the witch's name on it before.'

I believed it, but when, a score of years later, the time came for me to turn Esther's recital to advantage in a story, I boggled at the witchcraft, besides changing the milieu and giving Olwen's wickedness to her sister. None the less, some suspicion of Esther's active imagination remained in me. *Could* such a drama have happened? It is often useful to read newspapers, and over the years, following the writing of my story, I twice came across reports of doctors' errors similar to the one suffered by Olwen. In the second, a 'corpse' showed signs of animation in no less a place than a hospital mortuary in a thriving English town. The deposit of truth in all fantastic terrors bore fruit. Esther's tale had haunted me for long, a nightmare lobster scuttling in the mind's underneath.

Her far-away countryside was thick with happenings we did not experience in the Clydach Vale of 'D.A.', as our coal king was called. My copybooks often went disregarded. Sometimes Esther herself studied these with a ponderous intensity over my shoulder; she seemed to think we had better-quality teaching in the Rhondda than in her home fastness. She did not need to be told anything twice, and, my own scholastic help apart, she learned with express speed from my mother such matters as how to lay a ceremonious table or make light sponge cakes instead of the stolid *bara brith* of her upbringing. My mother thought her far the best servant we ever had. There had been three or four daily ones before, daughters of customers; each one had soon got married, and tribute to the domestic training they received from my mother was always rendered.

Esther showed a talent for drawing, too. It earned me a double lash of a cane in school. I had formed a practice of sketching picture frames around the arid arithmetical problems in my copybook; they were similar to those hanging on our walls, with frills and corner-knobs added. One day the teacher, Mr Vaughan, scrawled on a page, *Do not put frames around your work.* Esther noticed the command that evening. 'What's the matter with sums put in frames?' she protested. 'Take no notice.'

'He's got a cane,' I told her. Mr Vaughan liked using it too, and always on the palm, never on the less absorbent spaces of the covered buttocks. Jim Reilly, a recent friend of mine who had not been long in the Rhondda, complained of this to me, asserting that in Ireland the arse — a word as new to me as this boy from Ulster — was always the proper place. Jim had a compulsive need to grind dried green peas in his massive jaws and I used to take him a handful from the sack in our warehouse. They made him fart in the classroom, but that had nothing to do with his need; he was highly strung, though he did not look delicate.

'If it's frames your silly old teacher doesn't like,' Esther remarked, logically enough, 'something else let him have.' She took my pen, dipped it in the glass inkwell, and on a corner of the page where I had just completed a calculation, rapidly drew an owl-like head with extraordinarily large, stuck-out ears.

It was second-sight. She had never set eyes on Mr Vaughan, who lived two miles away in Llwynypia, and it was not until he called me to his desk, pointed to the drawing and asked me what it meant, that awareness of his outstanding ears penetrated my quickened mind. They had become scarlet. I mumbled that our servant had done the drawing. 'Well,' he snapped, reaching for the willow cane hooked on to the blackboard, 'you can pass these on to her with my compliments.'

Yet Mr Vaughan, our regular teacher in Standard 3, was accomplished at bringing our attention to wonders in history and geography. He encouraged us to grow hyacinth bulbs in narrow-necked green flasks of water; and one afternoon of rough wet, during our English lesson, he made me conscious of something obscure existing beyond his staid recital of a poem called *Meg Merrilies*. I bore him no malice for my undeserved caning. Besides, there had been a recent morning when a collier's wife, wearing her husband's cap (usually a sign of a truculent nature, whereas shawl-headed wives seemed gentler), had burst into the classroom and smacked his face for giving her little Ieuan a caning the day before.

It was a time when adult nerves were frayed in Clydach Vale. Another strike, of important dimensions on this occasion, lay in the wind. For me, strikes of the past were only talk — especially in connexion with my father's big ledger. Groups of Rhondda colliers idling all day on street corners had looked contented enough to me. (It was not in Clydach Vale that one week the men downed tools because they objected to a certain police-sergeant on the grounds that he had made a collier's wife into his fancy woman. The disliked sergeant was removed.) But this new strike was to become a bitter one. It lasted twelve months. It also drastically altered the disposition of our Esther, opened my own eyes a fraction, and caused my father to keep at the ready under his bed a gun he yearly took into the country for a few autumn days of pheasant and partridge shooting. It was the strike when nearly every shop down in Tonypandy was wrecked and looted by rioters and the cardinal error was made (by, it was long believed, Winston Churchill, the Home Secretary) of drafting armed troops into the Rhondda. While it happened it was little but enjoyable excitement for me; I learned all about its implications much later.

All the twelve thousand men of D.A. Thomas's Cambrian Combine pits in the Rhondda and Aberdare came out. D.A., though of a new breed of coal owners, a Liberal and a willing negotiator with the Miners' Federation, found he had become a villain. Earlier in his career he had refused to join the feudal Association of Mineowners, incurring its enmity, and when their men jibbed at conditions and struck, D.A. had welcomed many into his capacious Cambrian fold. He became very rich, and thought of himself as The Little White Father, a pleasing title for his power over the Cambrian share capital of two million pounds. He became prince of modern Wales, laying a fatherly hand on docks, railways, steelworks and newspapers, and in due time he was also able to lay a hand on German-owned property liquidated by the Board of Trade during the Kaiser's war, besides nourishing Great Britain as Food Controller in Lloyd George's Government.

But his recognition of the miners' federal rights had not cured all ills, and the men's everlasting dissatisfaction brought to us now, besides hundreds of unbelonging police, the invasion of troops, commanded by General Macready at strategic Pontypridd, Dr William Price's old stamping ground. D.A. had raged against his ingrates when an earlier, less drastic strike had begun; 'the men have struck the first blow below the belt. I am myself a man of peace, but there is, I fear, a little of the Old Adam left, and let not the men run away with the idea that the company will content themselves with silk-padded gloves, while they, the men, fight with knuckle-dusters. The men have come out without notice. They did not think it necessary to consult me first. But they will not return till we give permission.' In this short-time dispute the men obtained half the 20 per cent advance in pay they demanded.

The fighter held out against them for a fierce year now. He belonged by nature to the relentless old breed of the Association after all, men like Sir W.T. Lewis and David Davies of Llandinam. I had seen him, on his periodic visits to Clydach, riding up to his colliery at the far end of our vale. News would quickly pass that he was coming up the main road. His horse trotted slowly. I had expected, the first time, to see at least a frock coat and a topper. Except for his pince-nez, which flashed, he looked as casually everyday as my father on our horse. But D.A. was stern of face. He did not appear to notice anybody or anything in his kingdom, a man apart and alone, for all his rough cap like a collier's. Coal kings, although rich, sat lonely on fiery steeds. I did not know he had a daughter, the young woman who was to take the title of Lady Rhondda after his death; she was to find room in her paper, *Time and Tide*, for a couple of my stories about behaviour in such places as Clydach Vale.

The great strike began after D.A. had locked out 800 men from one of his lesser collieries in the Rhondda, the Ely. They had been disputing about the price list for a new seam of coal opened far below where the rest of us walked in the sun and rain. Following the lock-out, the South Wales Miners' Federation took a ballot, and called out all the 12,000 men of D.A.'s other pits. By the first day of November the Cambrian Combine strike was on. Then other coal-pits struck in sympathy; soon, 30,000 men were out, and foot and mounted police from Cardiff and elsewhere began to arrive. The soldiers came later.

Months of the strike had passed when one night I woke before dawn and heard a distant bugle call. The bugle hadn't wakened me. My parents had come from their room into mine, the long front room overlooking the main road. I saw them standing at one of the dim windows. A curtain was pulled aside an inch or two. There was a whisper of softly tramping feet in the road below, where the gas lamps were always extinguished hours before dawn by a man with a long pole. The bugle sounded again, more faintly. I went back to sleep.

It was not a soldier's bugle. Our Clydach Vale men, led by their agent Noah Rees, had been signalled thus to assembly. They planned to wreck the colliery powerhouse. They did not succeed. Extra police had been drafted to the colliery — it was said there had been a betrayer — and attacked the men at the bridge which approached the vital powerhouse. Not a man got through. I learned what the bugle and tramping feet meant when I listened to talk in our shop next day; and coarse-mouthed, but not coarse-natured, Jim Reilly told me that his bastard of a father had been in the fight and had a lump on his head the size of an egg out of a gander's arse, which he didn't know was a male one until I told him. Jim hated his father and took pleasure in telling me of the mishap. He did not complain at all of strike deprivations such as pocket-money. I liked him, preferring him to bossy Idwal, who had brought me such bad luck in Mrs Blow's pear tree. When the charity soup kitchens were opened in the schools for the strikers' children, and pea soup with chunks of beef in it was the most perpetual item, Jim said he hoped the bloody strike would last for ever. He had never eaten so well at home.

I was not eligible for the feasts in our school. We had enough food at home and did not lack cake throughout the strike. But debts grew and grew in our Ledger of Old Accounts. Tidy old customers could spare a few shillings out of Federation strike pay. But orders had to be cut down, or it was bankruptcy for us. My mother looked more and more harassed. My father stayed at home in the evenings. Before this strike, I had enjoyed what could be called neglect, which wasn't that for me. I had the public life of the shop, where there was always something going on. My father would draw up important letters for ignorant customers, especially those who were not chapel-goers and therefore could not consult a minister. He gave advice on legal matters and witnessed wills. Almost as many men as women came to the shop, and all of them talked. My father was such a talker that I stopped listening. His verbosity filled my mother with foot-tapping impatience; she had a constant cry of anguish — 'Come to the *point!*' It had no lasting effect.

She volunteered for the roster of noon service in the charity soup kitchens, and, on returning to the shop, always kept her flowered or fruited hat on all the afternoon. She liked the handsome big hats of the time, had many, and saw no reason to lower this flag during our bad time, except for not buying new ones in

Cardiff, or taking trips there. Life wasn't much changed at home. Esther would seldom venture out. Her brother, now that she was installed comfortably in her place, had stopped coming to see her, but once or twice she sent him half a crown at his lodgings. She was certain he would not take part in the rioting going on down in Tonypandy; he had been a chapel boy in Cardigan.

In all the twelve months our shop was not attacked and looted. But my father placed his gun under the bed. He put it there after Dai Morgan's slaughter-house below my school had been raided and set on fire one night. By that time the soldiers had come. Their holiday tents dotted a low mountain field above Llwynypia colliery, where another pitched battle with police had taken place; hundreds of rioters had attempted to storm the yard and reach the powerhouse, and were foiled again. Down in the pits of this colliery astute Sir Leonard Llewellyn, D.A.'s general manager, had left three hundred ponies, instead of bringing them up for strike-time grazing on the mountains, thus exciting great public sympathy for these forlorn animals alleged to be abandoned by the men; constant inquiries about their welfare from George V, fresh on the throne, added to the newspaper pity for them. In Tonypandy all the shops in long Dunraven Street were boarded up. Schoolchildren were forbidden to stray far, but roving towards Tonypandy with Jim Reilly one evening we saw a young man dashing through a back lane with a whole ham in his arms like a baby. We thought the police were in pursuit, would seize us too, and we sped in his wake until he threatened to kick our backsides if we didn't clear off. He must have thought we wanted a share of his ham.

Clydach Vale had remained comparatively quiet for a long time. The narrow, though long, cul-de-sac was not so easy for concealment or escape as the main valley. Our looters went down to Tonypandy. Then, as the second winter of the strike approached, we had our share of street battles. A tradesman suspected of revealing to the police a second plan for attacking the powerhouse of our colliery found his premises gutted. I saw his furniture and ledgers smouldering in the middle of the road. There was less looting now than retaliation against authority, especially against the soldiers, who in Tonypandy paraded the streets with fixed bayonets and were known to have given warning prods in a few scuffles with jeering gangs of men. The continued presence of soldiers brought bitter hatred and hardened the strikers.

Then, late one afternoon, came the battle that was to turn our Esther into a woman of full stature, brave and, after a time, faulty. I stood with her at one of our front windows upstairs. Below, in the locked shop, my father and mother remained on guard. A double row of policemen, two mounted sergeants at either end of them, had drawn up in the road outside the corner pub. An attack was expected. Marauding bands of rioters had been active for days in Clydach Vale, swooping on the police with taunting suddenness; they knew the lay-out of the back lanes better than these men drafted to the place from elsewhere. I was unaware then that my father had concealed in our stable the son of an old customer who was on the run after one of the brawls; it was not safe to tell schoolboys anything.

A mob was prowling in the nearby back lanes now. Fight was wanted, and nothing else. 'I can hear them,' Esther whispered, her hand gripping my shoulder. I couldn't. My first awareness of the quick attack was a huge noise of smashing glass. The window of Evans the butcher, only five numbers down on the corner of our side, had been stoned by men rushing from the sloped round at the opposite pub corner. They swarmed into view. '*Iesu Mawr!*' Esther breathed, gripping me tighter. I climbed on to the sill to get a better view, diagonally. We were safe from stones up here.

The road below mesmerized me. I was scarcely aware of Esther's grip and heavy breathing. Crammed with yelling strikers armed with sticks and mandrels, the road rose to my eyes. Policemen, far outnumbered, bounded among the rioters with batons drawn. The two horses reared. Their riders, one hand kept firmly on the reins, flayed long switches on to the rioters. I saw a helmet flying on to the porch steps of the pub, a rioter falling there, and a baton crashing down on his head as he attempted to rise. I heard a strange cry from Esther. Her grip left my shoulder.

She ran out of the room. Her flight down our back yard, then through the lane and round the corner into the main road, must have been done in record time. I saw her plunge into the mob, the only woman there. She whirled, ducked, fell to her knees, leapt up. I jumped from the sill and raced downstairs into the shop. My mother, arms folded, sat on a chair far away from the windows. The door-blind was down, my father peering from its side; he did not have the advantageous view of the corner battle that the upstairs window gave. 'Esther's fighting out there!' I shouted, and was not believed at once.

There was nothing to be done. It seemed only a minute later that Esther's hysterical cry came from our living-room, calling for my mother. By then the rioters had retreated round the pub corner, though several lay in the road, and were to be borne off to the police-station cells. In our living-room Esther lay on the sofa, blood coming from her mouth and streaking her neck. Her bright hair had fled its many pins and the lost diamanté back-comb my mother had given her at Christmas. Her frantic wailing was a revelation to me. It was my first experience of a woman demolished by emotional excess. I stood petrified until my mother, gathering the shining hair from the puffed face, told me to fill a bowl — 'lukewarm from the kettle,' she commanded, wonderfully calm; 'a sponge and a towel'. My father hurried in. 'She saw her brother hit by a truncheon,' my mother said. I heard it in bewildered respect.

'I saw him falling down,' Esther sobbed, more coherent now. '*Iesu*, I thought he'd been killed.'

That was not the only shock for her. There had been the horror of discovering that her brother was among the wicked men at all. Another shame made her cower now: she'd brought disgrace on us. Would the police come for her? My father said no, and this turned out to be correct. My mother sent her to bed. Esther descended from it in an hour and said she wanted to do some ironing. She had lost a tooth and thought it had 'gone down'. Her lip was cut and a knee grazed. A different kind of injury took some time to manifest itself. But she did not really question or upbraid herself for her action. If her brother had been killed she would somehow have gathered up the stocky corpse and borne it to safe keeping. Actually he had got away round the corner, and he was not prosecuted, as, over the months, some known rioters were. He scolded Esther for her interference. He said his pit butties would make fun of him.

Her decline began from this time. It obeyed the slow countrified rhythm natural to her, a contrast to her quickness of mind in picking up such essentials to living in the Rhondda as English speech and the wearing of frivolous clothes. For a long time I was not conscious that she had changed. Yet I reaped a new benefit from this different Esther who, when the strike was over, heartlessly kept a well-behaved young collier dangling on a string — a courtship in which none the less she made a last valiant effort to adjust herself normally to such an abnormal place as Clydach Vale.

The Cambrian Combine men lost their long struggle. They gave in to D.A.'s terms for return to work. But everybody knew their endurance now, and in the next strike they were to earn their reward. We had nearly two years of peace after the twelve-month dispute. And it was soon after our colliery began working that Esther allowed herself to be courted by a pit butty of her brother, a lodger needing to settle down in the usual way. His name was Gwilym. He had not taken part in any of the rioting, belonged to the Cambrian Male Voice Choir (eisteddfod winners in their day), and was afflicted with a patience which, had it not derived from the respected virtue love brings to some men, could be called wishy-washy.

To Esther his dogged wooing brought eighteen months of sombre procrastination, and if she did not really break a man's heart, this was because men's hearts in our heavily masculine world were not easily broken over baulked love. Silent about the courtship's preliminaries for some time, the whole affair bred an amount of strange humbug and evasions in her. I thought she spent her Wednesday evenings off at her brother's lodgings, where she was friendly with the landlady. Then one Wednesday she obtained my mother's permission to take me to the Empire Theatre in Tonypandy. I had not been there before; neither had Esther. In the street she whispered, 'You can keep your shilling for the seat. A friend will pay. But don't tell anyone, will you?' Her face had a hunted look under a straw hat decorated with flowers, and her person smelled of the carbolic soap which she believed had a safe-guarding property against nasty things — I came to realize presently that for her I possessed the same property on these occasions.

Outside the chemist's shop on Tonypandy Square, an area busy enough for the assignation not to be noticed, her young man viewed me with surprise. Esther gave no explanation to him, and he courteously accepted my presence. Wearing a stiff collar and tie instead of a criss-crossed muffler, he did not speak much, looking steadily ahead out of pale grey eyes. He asked my age before buying the Empire tickets, and I was allowed in for half-price. We sat on a long hard bench in the pit. Esther placed me between her and Gwilym. She kept her eyelids down as if they would never lift in such a place. The seats became packed. An attendant bawled 'Close up', and, tightly wedged between Esther's rigid thigh and Gwilym's warmly thick one, I was too excited to be bothered by the palpitating silence of the two courters. Great cerise curtains parted to reveal the only fairytale magic I knew in my upbringing. The play was called *A Royal Divorce*. I remember marble stairs in a garden and Napoleon's handsomely fat wife descending them in a trailing gown, real tears streaming down her pink cheeks, her crown off her head and dangling in a hand, so that there was no mistaking that her time was up.

It was the first of five or six such Wednesday treats. We saw the Carl Rosa Opera in *Rigoletto*, for which admission prices were doubled and no half-price. Gwilym did not jib; and I had extra pocket-money. We saw *The Bells*, *The Lights of London*, and *East Lynne*. One touring company distributed in the interval household utensils, baskets of groceries and toys to those who had lucky numbers on their admission tickets, which we hadn't. I always sat between the courters, and Esther's eyelids were always down, though she missed nothing. When we walked home, she told Gwilym outside our closed shop door, 'Next Wednesday,' nodded, and he stood there with a pinched smile until we vanished within. Proper courters went for their doting into the back lanes, where the mountain sheep wandered at night foraging for cabbage stalks and potato peelings. Allowing Gwilym to walk home with us after dark was Esther's only concession.

We were found out. A friend of my mother's had seen us twice in the Empire with the lovesick young man. Esther confessed, and my profitable chaperonage ceased. But my mother encouraged the courtship. She made it her responsibility to discover Gwilym's reputation. The report was sound. Esther, if inclined to choose a collier, couldn't do better. A first-class servant would be lost, but no doubt her married name would adorn a fresh double page of our black ledger; she and Gwilym would be trustworthy, teetotal and clean-minded.

Esther remained both inclined and not. Her Wednesday evenings became a privacy beyond my ken. But I was love's messenger for Gwilym, thus making some return for his Empire treats. He would hang about the colliers' gossiping corner opposite the

Central for hours, waiting for me to appear and take a folded scrap of paper to Esther. She would read the notes with a frown, and, never putting anything in writing for anyone, give me a verbal message to take back — 'Tell him I wasn't in a temper,' or, 'Say I don't like menageries or concerts'. I found myself with a contempt of Gwilym's abject slavery to a girl familiar to me as the horse in our stable. Once or twice I avoided returning to him with her message. On some Saturday evenings, still waiting at the corner, he would hand me a quarter-pound bag of her favourite sweets, Rowntree's fruit gums. She would count the sweets and give me exactly half; if there was an odd number I had the extra one.

But at last she took to going into our back lane with him on Wednesday nights. This promising move began more than a year after my Empire treats. I knew about it because she came in that way, sharp at ten o'clock, instead of by the shop door. But nothing was said. The courtship went on for a further long while without incident. Once Gwilym handed me a brooch in a tiny box for her. Esther gave it a shrewd glance, said he must have won it at a hoopla stall in the fair, and later handed it to the woman who combed the gigantic Cambrian waste tip for saleable bits of coal. My contempt of Gwilym increased. I felt certain that he had never fingered Esther's mysterious bush. However bad the winter weather he seemed to be waiting oftener at the corner, and I noticed his voice had become hoarse. Esther told me he had been missing choir practice. But he did not take to any drinking. This would have given her reason to arrive at the hard decision.

Her flat-iron, while I sat at the other end of the table on homework evenings, would plunge down with more force than she had supplied formerly, her gob of testing spit issue more virulently. She tended to talk of Gwilym oftener, and derogatively. 'He comes from North Wales,' she would say. Or, 'He plays quoits in that field down by the river.' Or even, 'He sings in the Male Voice Choir.' These criticisms seemed undeserved even to me. Months had gone by when she said, 'Your father says there's going to be another strike. The bums I might have in if I get married.' Few disgraces were more terrible than bailiffs removing household possessions. A crowd of sightseers would gather to view the dramatic act, news of it passing rapidly from street to street.

'We're always having strikes,' I pointed out, not displeased at the prospect of another. Esther shook out a rolled bodice with an impatient flapping, and I added, 'Gwilym can find someone else.' Our chapel was full of unmarried girls, most of them singing louder and sweeter than anyone else.

Esther drew herself up, her eyelids shooting up too. 'He wants *me*!'

The predicted strike came. It was a more orderly one this time, and, for a while, all our Cambrian men did not come out. Gwilym remained in work. Yet this promising sign was of no avail. One Wednesday night Esther returned as usual through the back lane. But this time she entered our living-room with drama in her face. Her bared eyes looked distraught as eyes that have seen the supernatural. Panic lay in them, as it had when she returned from among the rioters. My mother was in the living-room. After a hard swallow and a jerking back of her shoulder, Esther announced at once, 'I must go back to the country now'. It was a month's notice. She had come to decision at last. I heard no explanation of it. I did not ask her for one. Time was changing our old association, and I was to look at her with a new curiosity.

My mother attempted to make Esther think more carefully over the miserable retreat from courage. Herself critical of the coalmining life, none the less she had a deep admiration for most colliers' wives, and also (when she forgot the Ledger of Old Accounts) for the men's important struggles for better conditions and rewards. Besides, Esther hailed from a very poor Cardigan home; her farm-labourer father earned only eighteen shillings a week. My mother reminded her that there were plenty of other young men to choose from. But Esther would not budge. Her brother came to see her and failed in persuasions; and she refused to go out during the month's notice. Somewhere far away in me I felt an oddly welcome acceptance of her going. She departed with her roped tin trunk while — to my relief — I was at morning school.

It was a long time before I stopped missing her. My mother found a Clydach Vale girl to come in daily; she stole cocoa and soap from the shop, putting them up her elastic-edged knickers. We had three or four girls in quick succession, but not one was of the order of Esther, and each tried to impose her will on me by the usual method of accusation, to attempt to reduce confidence by inducing guilt. Except for a silver-frosted Christmas card one

Christmas, Esther did not write to us. When I thought of her I imagined her milking in some lonely green fastness where a policeman was rare as a butterfly on an iceberg. She wore a thick flannel skirt, checked shawl and stout boots as she trudged with two pails to the stone dairy of a whitewashed farmhouse tucked away on a hymn-pure hillside. She had forgotten all the English words picked up so nimbly with us. She would marry a farmhand who put an X to documents requiring his signature, as some country-born colliers did, asking my father to witness it.

I was wrong. It must have been three or four years later — the Kaiser's war had begun — when one September afternoon I arrived home from the intermediate school at Porth to which I had passed by then, and found a lady visitor seated at the tea-table with my mother. Under a wide hat containing a sharp-eyed bird with outspread wings, she sat with an erectness conveying not only the discipline of a lengthy corset but correct visitor's manners. She looked altogether dressily well-off. It was Esther. She had given a cry when I slouched in with my satchel hanging from a shoulder:

'He's grown!'

My adolescent embarrassment lasted throughout tea. I ate and drank in an agony of uncertainty. Formerly it was her eyelids that were nearly always lowered, and mine up; mine kept down now, and her eyes shone on me without stint. My fingering of her bush had returned. Again I heard her grunt as she turned over. Had she *known*? I could scarcely accept that I had done such an act to this well-spoken lady whose corset made a tiny noise of creaking as she leaned forward to take a piece of sponge cake.

'Esther is married now,' my mother had said, and they soon resumed talk appropriate to their mutual status.

She had married into Insurance. Her husband, much older than herself, was district superintendent for one of the impressive companies, his area in West Wales extensive. They owned a bay-windowed house in a Cardiganshire coastal town, well away from the unbridled sea. The Welsh husband bore the astonishing Christian name of Alfonso. He went to London four times a year, but Esther had never gone with him there. Perhaps it was effort to be his contemporary — even to my furtive glance her clothes seemed too old for her — that made her look fifty or more to me, thus deepening my embarrassment. There was even a slight trace of compassionate patronage of my mother. As a married woman Esther was not only her equal but lived immune to the insecurities of such a place as the Rhondda, our everlasting strikes beyond the aid even of Insurance.

'Alfonso,' she said, 'is always praising my sponge cakes.' This was a salutation to my mother.

'Alfonso can't be a Cardigan name,' my mother remarked.

'No. Belonging to his family it is. He says there was a Spaniard long ago that was shipwrecked in Cardigan Bay and married his great-grandmother. A long, thin nose my Alfonso's got, and hair black and shiny as a beetle, forty-five though he was last birthday. A mop of hair he's got like you don't see anywhere in Cardigan.'

I stared hard at my plate, listening. I did not hear of any children. Esther had come to Clydach Vale that day to visit the brother she had once attempted to rescue from policemen's truncheons; he too had married, and a child had been born the week before. Gwilym was not mentioned while I sat at the table; but I already knew he had left Clydach Vale, to work in Cwmparc pits. I gladly escaped into the shop when my father came in for a quick cup of tea, and when he returned I went out for a walk. Esther had left by the time I returned. In the manner of visitors coming from the country, she had brought us a present. It was a plucked duck, and, since the weather was warm, she had stuffed it discriminately with sage leaves and a quartered onion.

Six: Boys

Long before Esther paid us that visit it was not contrition or a wish to be redeemed that made me skulk into a revivalist meeting. It must have been some hunger deeper than ordinary curiosity of the wayward behaviour of grown-ups. Or perhaps it was only a retaliatory need to see them humiliated.

Gossip among boys is random, voracious and selectively narrowed to their interests. The ears of boys, pure as a hare's, pick up information useful to their rudimentary instincts and easily reject what is no concern of theirs. Boys mind their own business. Ignored by their elders where important things are concerned, or treated as short-weighted in the head, they gather necessities in their own loitering way. Words are picked up by the edges, pristine imagination gets to work like a dynamo, and it doesn't really matter if putting two and two together in this domain leads to error.

I had heard about the revival in our shop. A woman customer said that people were having their sins beaten out of them with sticks in meetings down in Tonypandy; and, lowering her voice, she mentioned a name known to me. It seemed to me behaviour worth investigation. I did not succeed in witnessing the ceremony on the evening I ventured into a meeting. But Bessie, an unmarried young woman said to have been shrived in that way, was to bring me round from a swoon the next day.

She was the elder sister of Gethin, a dull-witted boy in my school class. Gethin had worms just then. He scratched, ground his teeth, and had nightmares which he described to us. In a moping sort of way he bragged of his affliction, and said all the world had turned yellow as a canary. His sister, who must have been about twenty, moped in a different wretchedness and had more reason for it. Her unrequited love for the blacksmith in his forge opposite her home was well known. It was to take her off to the asylum.

She would sit for long stretches in the downstairs front window of her home, gazing out fixedly across the road to the forge in an open shed which Goronwy, who was under thirty, had taken over from his diabetic father. There, in addition to the hooving of horses, a steel fender or other hearth accoutrements could be ordered for a wedding gift. Goronwy, rhythmically hammering on his anvil all day, could be seen from the road in dark outline suddenly illumined by a shaft of flame. He seemed to take no particular interest in women so far, and was single without any talk about it. Bessie, sitting in her window, sometimes waved to me when I went past on my way home from school. Her white face made me halt without halting my steps.

Whether she had gone to her shriving in the revival to rid herself of her passion I did not discover. It was one of the little revivals, with no celebrated evangelist such as Evan Roberts to sweep it into fame and take all Wales into a magnetic spell. By the time I slipped into a Tonypandy hall to satisfy my base curiosity it had already dwindled. But there, as on every evening of the week, were those who still hankered for a solution of their lot. Everyone in the half-filled hall, except me, was fully grown. The service had begun. I sat alone on a back bench, ready to flee from any attempt to haul me into redemption. I only wanted to *look*. Jim Reilly had refused to go with me; he said they'd grab us. Several people turned to eye the very young seeker who came in late. I could not see Bessie there.

I waited. There was a shouting address from a strong-looking young man on the platform. I could tell that his *hwyl* was not good. After a lot of singing, the preacher invited us to go to the platform, one at a time. I sat up in expectancy. A man climbed the steps to the platform and gabbled words I could not sort out. A strange groaning rose from someone else in the congregation. Was that for which I waited about to begin? I had heard that a converted man or woman lay flat on the floor and was thrashed by two deacons in turn, while the people sang. I waited. Other groaners in the congregation, bass-voiced men and whimpering women, joined in. The man on the platform gabbled on; I could see his adam's apple jerking up and down. Then the evangelist passed a hand across his forehead; he fell quiet, and returned to his seat in the congregation. Another man climbed up. I knew there would be no caning. There was only hunger in that miserable hall. I stole out unheeded.

On the way home from school with Jim Reilly and others the next afternoon I took part in a battle with a gang from Standard 4. They chased us as far as the blacksmith's forge. We were pelted with stones. Goronwy shouted to us to clear off. A sudden stunning in my face felled me. I woke under a gush of water. Bessie had seen me on the ground from her parlour window and carried me into her kitchen with Jim Reilly. She held my head gently under the tap. 'Keep bending down,' she said, calm and sure. 'Nothing in a bleeding nose. You fainted, that's all.'

Jim, his duty done, ran off. Bessie's worm-infested brother waited unconcernedly for his tea. She gave me a cup when no more blood oozed from my nose. A smell like nightstocks came from her. There was no extraordinary sign of redemption in her smooth white face, and she spoke with a quiet, far-away exactness. I could hear the striking of the anvil across the road. The only strange thing Bessie did was open a Bible while I drank tea. She read out a psalm in her clear voice. Then she insisted on taking me home. It was my first time in their house, where nobody else was present then; and I did not go again. But I saw her often in the parlour window. She waved a hand, except on an occasion when she stared beyond me like a big white-faced doll sitting between the looped curtains. Then I saw her no more. She had gone to Bridgend.

Asylum: a flower of a word. But people didn't use it; they said 'Gone to Bridgend' instead. The building stood outside the distant Glamorgan town, and men and women who went there seemed never to come back. It was Bessie's brother, by then rid of his worms, who told me she'd gone to Bridgend when I asked him why she wasn't sitting at the window any more. 'Walking downstairs in the middle of the night,' he said, 'and shouting she couldn't hear Goronwy's anvil going any more.'

At Whitsun, after useless surgical attention to my broken nose, I was sent for a week of recovery to my religious grandparents in Ynysybwl. I had no worms, but night terror of a huge wardrobe of blood-red wood in my room at home afflicted me. Familiar pieces of furniture can speak, and this one was hostile to me. A spotted oval mirror in its centre panel held evil, the hanging clothes of grown-ups inside its thick silence were capable of walking out to dance a bodiless jig. I was imprisoned in a bottle, struggled vainly to get out of its slowly contracting neck, and the bottle rolled under the living wardrobe. I woke from my half-sleep to my own shouts. The wardrobe filled me with revulsion even in the daytime. I would not open it.

There was no wardrobe in my little room in Ynysybwl. It was the quietest house I had ever known, though the silence was dominated, upstairs and down, and night and day, by the portentous *tick tock* of a massive old grandfather clock standing below the staircase, an Ancient of Days. Like my chapel-deacon grandfather himself, it was a comely clock, the grey cheeks of its face painted with faded roses, its genital pendulum and dim weights visible within side-panels of glass, its gilded feet standing foursquare in its rightful home. Its *tick tock* at night, less a threat than a solemn warning, became related to the wardrobe at home, and I would bury my head under the blankets.

I did not like my grandfather, or my aunt and uncle who lived there. Only my grandmother pleased and did not perplex me. It was she who, at long last, persuaded my mother to discard my flannel shirts; it was she who, in my uncle's salad days, used to creep down from bed and unfasten the door bolted against the drunkard by my chapel-pillar grandfather. She could speak fluent English and, like my mother, had been an uncertificated school-teacher, and she had known Dr William Price's heyday exploits in nearby Pontypridd. My grandfather's English words were few; perhaps because he was a thinker, his spoken Welsh was meagre too. My spinster aunt, fat with flesh and reproof, was rid of all feeling for children; when she came to live with us at Clydach Vale, after my widowed grandfather remarried in the Pontypridd registry office without telling any of his family, she persecuted me. Later I wondered if the wily old deacon, marrying a buxom widow-member of his chapel, did not mind distressing this daughter. But my mother, his favourite, had wept for ten minutes into a large towel on hearing the astonishing news.

Cleanly regular in his habits as his clock, he understood money and owned several houses in Ynysybwl. He was a respected overman in the small, family-owned colliery which still kept semi-rural Ynysybwl in a feudal condition of peace; they seldom had strikes. He was treasurer of his thriving chapel too. Yet his only son, soon after entering the pit, had taken to drink. The father dispatched him to Canada; the son begged to come back; the price of return was a signing of the pledge. The pledge was kept, and my uncle sank into black sheep redemption. A family disgrace, he sat at the table in scowling blankness. But he was as censorious of me as my aunt; I represented their successful sister, battling away in the wicked Rhondda. When I burst into meaningless laughter at that severe table one Sunday, my uncle's bald eyeballs rolled to me. 'Only fools laugh,' he growled. It penetrated, a curiosity of the alien world of grown-ups. How could I know that this prodigal son, who never married, should not have been redeemed? I only knew he had no use for me.

My grandmother made efforts to entertain me. She sat in a rocking chair and often smiled. Their opulent chapel had been built in more palmy days than our chapels in the Rhondda. Its purple-lozenged windows steamed with exudations of anthems and justified hallelujahs. God was solid there. Nobody was in debt. The women sat in Sunday splendours of feather boas and top-price best, the men glistened with mammon securities, and the great heaps of money in the wooden collection plates surprised me. At the evening communion service four silver wine cups and four silver dishes of bread cubes, brought to the crowded pews by eight deacons, glittered in the unstinted light of jets from gas brackets encrusted with gilt foliage. The women tucked their spotted face-veils up over their nose-tips to eat and sip, licked their lips in delicate satisfaction, and lowered the veils. This chapel stifled me even more than Gosen in Clydach Vale. My grandmother said to me that night, 'Well, you're not like a boy we've got. He was offended by only grown-ups having the communion, and one evening when the plate went by him he fetched a crust of bread from his pocket and pecked away like a pigeon.' I could tell that she kept God at a judicious distance and would not use Him for her own ends. But her quiet husband was boss of the house, and the unspoken punishments in his private bible frightened me.

I did not want to go to prosperous Ynysybwl for a whole week again. Relations were best for once-a-year days like Bank Holidays. But the visit refreshed me for the Rhondda. The newly-arrived tramcars swept up and down our ten hard miles; some families took a picnic basket to the top deck on Bank Holidays, staying up there for a couple of to-and-fro journeys lasting hours. A man in Clydach Vale went off his head and walked the main road naked, carrying a pet Angora rabbit by the ears; he was taken to Bridgend. Bums cleared into a van the contents of a schoolfriend's home and he slept on a floor mattress and ate meals at an upside-down tea chest given him by my father. I won another deserved medal for sprinting at the summer school sports held in Coronation Field on top of a mountain cracked from pit subsidences. Half of a colliery waste tip on the side of another mountain up the main valley broke away one wet dawn — 'It came away clean as a slice of Christmas pudding,' declared the only spectator, who dashed to a signal box of the railway below. The half roared down without mishap to anyone.

In Clydach Vale we had The Flood. Nobody had taken notice of the old sealed level piercing far into a lower slope of a mountain above rows of houses and a chapel and another school in that high part of the vale. It had been one of the pioneering coal-yielding levels, abandoned after the Cambrian colliery opened, and the thread of water always trickling from a low chink in its walled-up entrance went disregarded. One afternoon a roar was heard from this evil throat of the mountain. The sealed entrance had burst and a gigantic spout of black water hurled out, gathered impetus down the slope, demolished three terrace houses, bombarded the chapel, swept across the main road, flooded the full school, and found partial outlet in a steep gulley leading to the river. It poured for half an hour. Colliers going home from a shift heard the roar and reached the school in time for rescue. A baby, carried down from the smashed terrace houses, was snatched dead out of the swirl, and there were other dead. We were kept back in our school until the waters abated. With Jim Reilly I raced up to the burst level, going through back streets; a shallow river still lapped through the main road. We saw a stream of acid water coming from the floor of the jagged hole, quietly enough now. In the gaping middle of the terrace below a brass bedstead hung from a broken room. There was an acrid smell of the mountain's inside.

The nine who lost life were buried in a great ceremonious funeral, there were benefit concerts for a fund, and for a long time afterwards memories were dated from before or after The Flood. But deaths and disasters belonged more properly to the colliery. A horse-drawn brown van, carrying either a dead or badly injured man, passed through our streets slowly. According to the burden within, it would stop at a house or go on to Llwynypia hospital. News of its approach brought people out to watch its soft-tyred amble. Would it go into a side street, draw up before a chosen house, bring forth a dead man? Its errands were frequent. Only those men with silicosis did not need it. Their blight was more laborious, long nights coughed away. Far over the mountains lay the Home for bad cases. It did not have the hushed reputation of the Bridgend asylum, but there were affiliations with the melancholy sum of a life resolved.

The pits were working full time now. Saturday nights burst with the vigour of a big explosive cabbage. Pairs of Rhondda constabulary, always taller and wider than policemen elsewhere, patrolled the streets in strong-jawed readiness, silver chains looping their bucket helmets. Shops, open until midnight in good times, gained lost ground. The pubs sang and shouted with language. Enmities were settled on the road outside, until the canvas stretcher from our five-celled police station bore off the one too far gone to care whether he was victor or not.

The Central was the most popular of our seven pubs in Clydach Vale. Jim and I, challenging each other to nip a mouthful of beer from some laid-down mug in the closely-packed bars, would dart in and out on Saturday night. I was caught only once, a collier gripping me by the hair and, while Jim, fled, forcing the remainder of his pint down my throat, and I liked the forgiveness of all things and people that followed. But the ill-lit side cave for women was forbidden territory; only a quick peep round the ever-closed door was possible. On two facing wall benches slouched a dozen colliers' wives in saturnine conclave. They were clever at going in and leaving without being seen.

Mrs Hughes Number 8 was an exception. She sat in the cave every Saturday night until a quarter to eleven, then, like a blowzy actress blown up for her part, crossed the road to our shop to more or less pay her week's account, order more victuals, and boldly tell everybody that she had managed six pints of stout. She would borrow half a crown in the arid middle of the week and get it put down in our day-book as a food item. Surprisingly, she was frightened of her half-size but watchful husband, and, as surprisingly, my mother much liked this hard-drinking woman. She hailed from Bristol slums.

She had eight tremendously eating sons, six of them already in the pits, and, as if logically, she lived in 8 Pleasant Terrace. Everybody called her Mrs Hughes Number 8, and she did not grieve that no daughter had come to bless her. 'I've got eight men and a husband to feed,' she would say to other customers, buying four pounds of sliced bacon and three large tins of tomatoes for their Sunday breakfast. In midweek she looked subdued to much less than her Saturday night size, and, after peering furtively up and down the road, would whisk into our shop for her half a crown. Yet when a Bristol relation died and left her £100 she wiped off her strike debt in our ledger; and in the Lord's good time began a fresh one.

Her overgrown last-born, who was my age, was a man to her. 'He eats as much as the others though he's so short-sighted,' she alleged. 'He can't wait to go down the pit.' But she lost him. He died of peritonitis after a last-minute operation for appendicitis; his pains had been wrongly diagnosed by the clumsy doctor who ruined my nose. My mother thought it fitting that I should attend his funeral, instead of my father. It was my first funeral. I arrived at the house a few minutes before it set out and saw Mrs Hughes sitting, upright and apart, on a hard chair in the crowded living-room. The coffin lay in the front parlour. All the people, bustling about until the chapel minister arrived, ignored her. She wanted nobody. Ceaseless tears splashed down her face from wide-open eyes that stared at nothing. Not one of the experienced women neighbours preparing the repast for returned mourners, not one of the seven sons ranged there in stiff black, or her small, deprecating husband, approached her. They knew she had reached the source of grief and must remain there alone for a time. But she was the central fact in the room, monumental, and not to be erased from memory.

One of her sons, noticing my embarrassment, smiled at me and said, 'You will walk with us behind the coffin.' There were no carriages. The flower-decked coffin was carried on a worn bier by four men, relieved by others half-way on the two-mile walk to Trealaw. No women attended. There was singing outside the house, but none on the route; in these bygone ceremonies, burial of the young was always more hushed than for those who had been able to make more clamour in life. The walk to Trealaw was a long discipline for me, unknown before.

It was drinking men, rather than the few ditto women, who roused my mother's irritation with the place. They did it on a much grander scale than women. I saw her give ruthless vent to her irritation late one Saturday night. A model customer stood settling his week's account in our full shop. He belonged to the tribe of unmarried young lodgers who, since Victorian days, had come seeking fortune in the deceptive valley and who, normally, found a local wife and established a dynasty. This one was nicknamed The Gentleman Collier. There was no other like him. His landlady said he owned nine pairs of shoes which he polished as no shoes had ever been polished. He wore smart jackets of maroon or green velvet, fanciful neckwear, kid gloves, and no hat or cap on his long, carefully arranged Botticelli hair. Mrs Bowen Small Bag, the midwife, declared him a credit to the place. He was judged to have come from either England or America, but there was no traceable accent in his melodious diction. Working on the coalface in Number 1 pit of the Cambrian, he preferred the unfavoured night-shifts. He always chose his own groceries, his landlady cooking for him.

It was approaching eleven o'clock when another lodger-customer, a bantam man swollen with Saturday-night bombast, lurched into the shop. Several excrescences always on his inflamed face had caused him to be nicknamed Jenkins Warts. A thickset, two-rooted beetroot of a man, for a moment he eyed the debonair Gentleman Collier with a lurking belligerence, suddenly gripped a fistful of his velvet jacket and gave him a push against the counter, behind which my mother stood.

'I'm as good a man as you are!' he bawled, and struck a fighting stance. All business stopped for a silent instant. I stared entranced from the coffee machine, where I had been turning the handle.

Years of exasperation against bad times, unpaid debts and meagrely rewarded hard work galvanized my mother. Before her lay the day-book, a sizeable volume from which the unpaid cash totals of daily purchases were transferred to the sombre Ledger of Old Accounts. She lifted the book in both hands, leaned forward, and brought it down smartly on the bantam's capped head. '*Out!*' She pointed a finger to the door. He slunk away at once. Struck by a woman!

The Gentleman Collier adjusted his tugged jacket into its former drape. 'Gone too far even for the Salvation Army, poor chap!' he observed. My mother took a pencil from her coiled hair and reopened the day-book. 'Let me see, that clears up everything for your week, doesn't it? Eighteen shillings and fourpence.' She was as instantaneous with sums as with logical deductions.

Jenkins Warts was lost to us as a customer, and his debt from the last strike remained unpaid. One Sunday morning, a fortnight after the Saturday night clouting, my father found a thick tail of tar running in a congealed stream from inside the letter-flap of our shop door, spent matches scattered below it.

Jim Reilly remained my close friend until he left our school to go down the pit and I left to go on to the 'County' in Porth, which made a change of position inevitable. Jim found life tedious in school, and often out of it. But he was clever at offsetting this; and also borne up by his cursing warfare with his father. His habit of chewing dried peas had stopped by the time we formed another one together. We would go in search of front windows draped all over with white bedsheets or tablecloths. That winter we roved through the streets as far as Llwynypia and Penygraig. It was his idea. He was the one who knocked at the door and, his face very polite and humble under his shining blond fringe, ask if we could pay our respects. It was normal in colliers' families to allow any grown-ups to view the laid-out. We were denied only once, and then it was because the body wasn't ready — 'Come back tomorrow,' an old man told us. People were impressed by this tribute from boys in knickerbockers and school caps. Sometimes the body lay neat in a coffin on trestles in the front parlour; more often in a bed upstairs, which it was a triumph to penetrate. We viewed a dozen or more corpses that winter. On one occasion it was a candle-lit baby, from whose white, white face a silent woman drew away a piece of black-edged notepaper.

Our forays were of aid to the itinerant glazier called The Wandering Jew. When we came across him plying the streets we could tell him where he would find a cracked window-pane. Nobody knew his proper name or where he came from. A heavy frame of panes roped to his back, putty and cutters in the pockets of his ragged coat, he tramped over the mountains in all weathers, a battered man who looked very ancient to us. He was bent and he trudged and trudged. Where did he live? Why didn't he take the trams with his load of glass? We did not like to ask. He spoke in a slow, deep-down voice, gazed at us from a knowledge in his deep-set eyes which we could not fathom, and he seemed to respect boys as dignified persons who were old as himself. We saw him and his square frame outlined one evening against the darkening sky as he reached a mountain brow on his slow return to wherever his abode lay. Jim, who was not very bright in school, said he lived in Jerusalem.

Jim would often lapse into vague reveries. Then prim absences into the privacies of a girl clouded the freckled, strong-chinned face under his fringe of yellow hair. One August afternoon, a few months before he left school to go down the pits, at fourteen, we went searching for bilberries in the rough grass of a mountain top. Failing to find any of the luscious purple fruit, Jim sat down and, bored, unbuttoned his knickerbockers and showed me what he had. It was very fat and seemed a burden to him. 'In Ireland,' he said morosely, 'they give us stirabout.' He had seen his father's when the old bastard stood washing pit dirt off before the kitchen fire — 'It's smaller,' he added. His mother, a shouting virago who did not let any visitor into their house, would put her head round their front door and bellow into their street, 'Jim! Come home! *Jim!*' She could be heard beyond the street. He would run.

He went down Number 2 pit of the Cambrian. He told me his mother shortened an old pair of moleskin trousers belonging to one of his two brothers, and, philosophic about everything save his father, he accepted this and all his lot without complaint. I did not leave our school above the slaughter-house until after the next term. Meanwhile I saw much less of Jim; as a collier boy his way of life was different. I had been a pupil in the County school two years when, arriving back one afternoon, I was told about the brown van taking him home some hours earlier. He had been killed by a fall of roof. It would not take shape in my mind. Refusal of it remained locked in me. I could not go and knock at the door of his window-shrouded house to offer my respects. I dreaded seeing the white-draped windows. But I stayed home from school on his day and, at the last moment, sped up to the house for the second funeral I went to.

Seven: The Odyssey

Mr Samuel, M.A., the headmaster, had a thunderous presence tempered by far-sighted patience. Despite his ribboned pince-nez and gown and mortarboard I identified him presently with Homer. The sweep of his glance over the low pince-nez as he read morning prayers could bring all his fidgety little troops to order. He boomed, and he gave dignity to the motive of our attendance at his superior establishment.

Only once was I addressed privately by him. Alone in the washroom, parting my long flat hair before the mirror, his sonorous voice pronounced from the door: 'Boy, if you put tap-water on your hair you will be bald before you are thirty.' He passed on. His mortarboard was not on his own beautifully thick silver hair. Did he go out to wash it in our pelting rain?

We paid money to attend the 'County' then: a sovereign a term. Lessons included Latin and a choice of French or Welsh. Punishment was more subtle than from the Clydach Vale cane; we had repetitious copying of a long, long passage of literature. And there was the delivery, inescapable as the approach of a policeman's tread, of a terminal Report to parents. A boy could be expelled. We had cricket and a badged cup which cost half a crown; we paid for textbooks. Prim behaviour was expected of boys in the Porth County School. I was the only boy from Clydach Vale during my first term.

Walking the three miles home at four o'clock, to save the tram-fare for other purposes, I often went into Trealaw cemetery. It ran parallel to the main road from Porth. Tombstones brought a sense of repose at day's end, tasks done. It was surprising how many of the stones sealed a man, woman or child I had known by sight or talked to. Their set ages, from which they would never budge, gave me a sense of advantage too. Sometimes there would be a late funeral to witness. I stole a porcelain flower from under the smashed glass shade of an everlasting wreath; and took it back the next day.

We had different masters for different lessons. My eighteen-penny new copy of a prose translation of episodes in the *Odyssey* lay one day on my desk, an unopened square with buff linen covers. Because the English master was in hospital for an operation, Mr Samuel took the lesson for Form 1. He gave us an introductory talk about the Trojan war and the sore adventures of over-heroic Odysseus on the way home to his over-noble wife, neither of whom delayed my attention. Then Mr Samuel rose from his stool at his desk. He fixed his pince-nez more firmly and shook out his black gown, like an orator taking up position. It seemed for his own pleasure that his booming voice read an excerpt from the *Odyssey*. Nearly everybody in the class was stilled. I was stilled.

It was from the *Book of the Dead*. At the frontiers of the world, beyond the poplars of Persephone's Grove, the wanderers came to the River of Lamentation and the helpless dead rose out of the mist to greet the fortunate Odysseus. They sipped of the slain lamb's blood, gained strength, and held colloquy with him across the red trench. Some of them were long-winded for ghosts. Of them all, it was the tremendous name of Agamemnon that, for some reason, crashed most chillingly about my ears. Marble and fire shone in it. Why did his wife Clytemnestra even refuse to close his eyes and mouth after her fancy man killed him, with her help? His testy advice to Odysseus not to trust overmuch any wife impressed me. But years were to pass before I saw the Aeschylus play acted by the youths of Bradfield College at their Greek theatre and I heard bloodstained Clytemnestra, double axe in hand, give full-throated voice against the conceited wickedness of Troy's victor and his showy return from evil war. She reminded me of the draped woman poised above the Old Bailey dome, scales in hand.

I could not be parted from my *Odyssey*. It was always in my satchel on my way home, to be read in bed by candlelight. The obscure thing that had pricked my mind when I heard *Meg Merrilies* recited in the elementary school became a more decided quickening. The world opened into known old countries and islands on vast blue seas presided over by basic gods it would be perilous to forget. I began to admire over-admirable Odysseus. Agamemnon, his mouth open, was a monster grey fish slain not far from the shore of a sea purpled with spilt blood. Clytemnestra was a Suffragette. We had a few of them in the Rhondda, not much tolerated by the colliers or other men.

When our English master returned after his operation he did not have the oratorical magic of Mr Samuel. For him the *Odyssey* was no more than the term book set for thirty routine boys. But he awarded me nearly top marks for a terminal essay on any episode in our pruned *Odyssey*. I chose the Circe adventure. Most of the other boys, too, favoured the beautiful witch and her interesting habit of turning men into swine. Our master jotted under my 90/100: 'Very good, except that Homer does not mean us to admire the swine. Bear in mind they wept in the sties.' Apart from the English lessons, I paid little attention to other subjects and sank towards the bottom of my class in my end-of-term Report, then and thereafter.

The *Odyssey* was not enough. Of our thick books at home most had been unopened by me. A hefty volume called *The Casquet of Literature* contained swarms of excerpts; of them all it was the murder scene in *The Duchess of Malfi* that best whisked the Rhondda world away. I soon knew pieces of it by heart:

> What would it pleasure me to have my throat cut
> With diamonds? or to be smothered
> With cassia? or to be shot to death with pearls? ...

The oyster shell of a boy's mind is forced open at random. Or he reaches to what he wants with a crab's oblique approach. I did not share my tastes with anyone; for street companions I preferred the simple boys who could even be called rough, and rarely discovered them to be rough. I took to reading books beyond my station in life. At fifteen I found Zola, Flaubert, Anatole France and others of like dosage. They became of more interest to me than the Kaiser's war which, however, had meaning because it brought prosperity to our collieries and therefore to my home. But still there was one strike. General Smuts came down to plead with the unpatriotic men at a meeting in the Empire Theatre and, advised by Lloyd George to invite them to sing to him, succeeded in his persuasions.

I knew of the branch library in the front room of an ex-collier's house close to my home. It was run by the South Wales Miners' Federation. The librarian's job was his compensation for losing a leg in a pit accident. Persons not employed in the pits could borrow one book a week on payment of a shilling every three months. There was a long, glass-fronted bookcase, unlocked two evenings a week, when necessary. I never saw a woman in the room, seldom a man, and nobody of my own age. When I walked in to join, the peg-legged librarian stumped ill-temperedly into the room and gave me a distrusting look. He was obliged to let me join, but kept an eye on me as I scanned the packed bookcase he grudgingly unlocked.

'We don't keep books for boys,' he said. By that time I was in long trousers.

Among the many names of authors unknown to me were Marx, Engels, Bakunin and Tolstoy. Their books looked as if they never went out. Those by Marie Corelli and Hall Gine were shabby. I do not know what rationalist person selected the books, but translated French novels abounded. On my first visit, harried by the librarian's suspicion, I quickly chose a Zola, attracted by the exotic name and the title, *Drink*. The surly librarian entered its particulars in a ledger, and I signed receipt of it in a margin. He remained suspicious of my motives throughout my couple of years' support of his calling. I read *Madame Bovary*, many easy Anatole France works in large red volumes, Eugène Sue's exciting *Mysteries of Paris*, full of dramatic sewers, and, ringing in the mind clear as a bell, *Candide*, surely one of the most nourishing books for wholesome boys ever written.

The procession of half-comprehended characters retreated down my mind's corridors, shutting doors behind them, leaving obscure messages in their wake. I ploughed through *Anna Karenina*, and the mournful excesses of women in love became a solid fact; whenever a train ground into Tonypandy station for my holiday-time trips to Cardiff and elsewhere I saw defeated Anna throwing herself under its wheels. In Cardiff market-hall gallery I picked up for sixpence secondhand books in an alcove next to one for livestock. Strangest of all was a small green volume of translations from Baudelaire, the poems full of enticing taints and mildews, diseased lovers expiring on divans, melancholy acceptances of anguish and decay. The verses winged about the mind, peculiar birds, and went moping into cotes.

Snatches from the vast estate of poetry, gathered then and later — and poetry yields its rewards best in remembered snatches, especially if one is occupied with prosaic transactions unrelated to it — remained for ever. There were scraps from the springtime of the world:

> I, Hermes, stand here at the cross-roads
> by the wind-swept orchard, near the
> grey coast, offering rest to weary men.
> And the cold clear water gushes forth.

Or, from a sixth-century Welsh poet, the lament of Heledd for her brother after the English had sacked their mansion and slain him:

> Cynddylan's hall is dark tonight
> no fire no bed
> I'll be still when these tears are shed ...
>
> Cynddylan's hall's forlorn tonight ...
> O death why do you leave me here?

I began to take lonely walks late at night. I liked winter best. Hard winter in our high altitude, especially if there was moonlight, rang with a brilliance of stars throbbing in strange rhythm with the breathing mountains. In the clarity of the air with its everlasting touch of celtic green, the narrow vale, often deserted at that hour, acquired a sculptured form, a diamond-hard permanency. The big, troublesome colliery with its frail headstocks was a black smudge that would be wiped away.

One night I stood beside a steep gully down which poured a mountain brook, the water bright as frost. Below, the stone terraces of dwellings, set at exact angles, were beautiful and secret. Everybody was asleep in hoary night. Far ahead, where the vale closed in, reputed Roman steps cut a mountain; nearer, knobbed on an eminence, was the large, smooth, egg-shaped rock which might have known druidic sacrifices. From the icy moon came the living green of a cat's eye. The water dashed and sang, an unceasing voice of the past and future. I stood inside an awareness. It was one of those rare moments of interfusion that bring neither conscious happiness nor peace, and contain both. They bear the embassage that we are always alone, never without firm identity, and the world is ours. I was not to experience a similar visitation of ripeness again until ten or eleven years had gone, and I lay one evening under craggily towering cliffs beside the Mediterranean, resting there as I walked most of the way back to my Nice lodgings after winning some needed money at Monte Carlo. The god touches our shoulder seldom.

Other shades of Wordsworth's prison-house began to lift from the growing boy. I found a less guilt-ridden religious creed when I insisted on transferring my worship from Nonconformist Welsh-speaking Gosen chapel to the Anglican Church of St Thomas. It was High, with plenty of robes, pomp and incense. It also possessed a surprising preacher in its vicar, the unsung Reverend Meredith Morris, author of books on Welsh literature and on violin-makers. On Sunday evenings, his best times for giving vent, I would keep my eye on the clock at home; after the scandal which followed one of the vicar's sermons it had become necessary to arrive early at church if one wanted an advantageous seat close to the pulpit.

His attempts at *hwyl* were not successful. The inspired chanting did not lend itself convincingly to the English language. But he was a true-born actor, and one Sunday, in lieu of a sermon, he read us Maeterlinck's *The Blue Bird*, performing all the parts with adroit change of tone, sex and age. Sometimes, as if the pill-box pulpit was too small for his more obstreperous performances, he descended the steps and walked up and down the aisles among us. His discourses never alarmed me, and, long free of my flannel shirts too, I sat comfortably well-disposed to God.

A Sunday or two after the sweetness of *The Blue Bird*, Meredith Morris provided the sermon that was to gain for him thereafter an even fuller church, winning many Nonconformists from the chapels and other persons too lackadaisical to wash and change and set out for worship. In this sermon he had roundly attacked the vindictive God of the Old Testament, and, after reading a verse from the second chapter of Malachi, he hurled the Bible to the pulpit floor, raging, 'Are we to believe that a loving God would want to smear shit on people's faces?' A pause was allowed for the horrified silence in the church to accomplish its work; then the doughty soldier for Christ, picking up the Bible from the floor, resumed his argument more moderately.

On the following Sunday evening accommodation could not be found for everybody. Chairs and benches were brought from the vestry. People stood at the back. Mounting the pulpit, the Reverend Meredith Morris read the text for his sermon, then said, 'I understand we have a spy of the Bishop of Llandaff here tonight.' He descended from the pulpit and, gazing penetratingly along each crowded pew of regulars and non-regulars, walked the aisles.

Nobody was selected for a special scrutiny. The gesture was enough: he would stand no nonsense on his own territory from anybody. Had someone sent a letter to the bishop? The scandal over that awful word died down. But St Thomas's prospered. Soon, a spacious transept was built for the increased seekers after truth.

One Palm Sunday, purple-robed and accompanied through the streets by scarlet-cassocked boys on foot, our magnificent vicar rode to morning church on a mule, a sheaf of palm leaves in his arm. In his sermon that evening he told us of a recent trip to London. The crescendo was a performed description of one of the great religious paintings in the National Gallery. He became the painter as well as the painted figures. He crucified himself, arms outstretched against the white wall, head dropped in agony; on his knees, he became the weeping Magadalene and the Virgin. A glory of colour bathed the pulpit. The picture was there. I was to find Ruth Draper no better in the close of her Italian church item.

An Etty oil painting, bought by my mother, had been the first picture I saw clearly before this. She went off to a Cardiff auction sale one afternoon with the wife of a cousin who was a J.P. and miners' leader living in Pontypridd, and she came home with the framed painting. It was entitled *Cupids Arming*. Two buxom little boys of satiny rose flesh girded themselves with quivers and gilded shields, a faintly baleful expression of self-satisfaction on their innocent faces. A contrast to our black engravings of reproving biblical subjects, at which nobody looked, its colours and subject delighted me. I wanted to become a painter.

Eight: Spats and a Malacca Stick

Save for one or two local mining disputes, the war brought years of solid peace. It was the last truly golden era of the might of coal. While hostilities proceeded afar, colliers worked overtime. An English legend grew that a piano which nobody could play, and also a fur coat, entered every collier's home in the ill-famed valley. Pianos and fur coats, if any, were earned and deserved. I saw none. Pianos were rare at any time in the poky dwellings. But there was some extra money now. Our boss, D. A. Thomas, found his parliamentary career rewarded too, his compatriot Prime Minister appointing him Food Minister; he became Viscount Rhondda. In our valley there was no great shortage of victuals, especially of the basic collier's necessities, cheese and *cig moch*; extra rations were allowed for pit workers. Some of the debts in my father's Ledger of Old Accounts were wiped off; but many others belonged to customers gone to where there are no strikes or personal fecklessness.

Now that I was of reliable age, I deputized occasionally for my busy father in his Monday evening collections of debts and weekly orders from certain old-established customers in the far reaches of Clydach Vale. It was in the nature of social visiting. Between six and eight o'clock, with the day-shift men back from the pits, the families would be gathered in their bustling, hot living-rooms, the remains of a substantial meal on the tables. Usually a stout wooden tub stood before the fireplace, kettles and pans of hot water on the hobs. Pit-head baths were yet to come. A jet-black father and, if any, his sons, took their wash-down in turn, kneeling before the tub or standing in it, a wife or daughter called to wash the dull thick black coating from back and shoulders. Foot-long bars of our Sensation soap, cut into segments, hardened in a wire basket hooked under the warm ceiling where clean shirts and underwear hung from a wire square.

There was always a huge fire all the year, and always welcoming room for a caller, with a cup of tea if needed, and seldom any temper displayed before visitors. The Evans family, living at the windy top of the vale, close to the colliery, was my favourite. My last port of call, it was there I took a cup of tea and settled for a spell, the collected money and an order book in my school satchel. Mrs Evans, a large, housebound woman, recited her long order, pausing to consult her two daughters, who never married, while Mr Evans or Watkin, the full-size son, splashed naked in the round tub, bawling for warmer water, and the goose-bosomed daughters darted through the firelight, flung towels about, or cleared dishes noisily into the corner sink. It was a tight little stronghold of established family unity, and I did not sense any dissatisfaction lurking under the security. I was a belated sixteen.

Miss Ceridwen, living down the street, trotted in on one occasion, just as Watkin stepped into the tub after his father. Mr Evans stood on the rag-mat towelling himself; the son covered his privates with one hand, the other hand soaping his chest. A committee woman who had once spent a year in America, Miss Ceridwen was actively small of stature and an important noise in a popular Baptist chapel in that area. 'I've come about Elijah,' she announced, removing a sheet from the roll of posters she carried. 'You'll stick this on your front window, Mrs Evans?'

She held the sheet up. It announced a performance of Mendelssohn's *Elijah*. Heading the list of soloists was not a man's name, but that of Madame Jane Ellis-Roberts, with *London, Milan* and *Pontypridd* printed in brackets under it. 'Is *she* singing Elijah's part?' asked one of the daughters absently, gazing critically at the poster after pouring more hot water into the tub. Her father pulled on a shirt.

'It's a man's part, Morfydd *fach*.' Miss Ceridwen opened her handbag and took out a wad of vari-coloured tickets. 'The chapel will be full for this concert. No complimentary or half-price this time, because of her.'

'I thought she had retired a long time ago,' Mrs Evans remarked, stoning damsons at the table.

'She can be relied on. Two items she's singing, in the Miscellaneous after the interval. Only Part I of *Elijah* we are doing. How many tickets for you?' Miss Ceridwen briskly snapped off an elastic band from the wad. 'Three-and-six top price for this concert, then two-and-six, and a shilling the four back rows.' She looked at everybody in turn.

Except for Watkin sluicing water over his front, there was silence. Nobody wanted to go to this concert. Mrs Evans said finally, 'The concert is not till November. We'll see.' Her quiet husband reached for his trousers from a rod above the fireplace, and Morfydd vigorously washed her brother's back with a piece of flannel.

Miss Ceridwen's quick eye returned to me. She knew who I was and why I was there, with my satchel of money. 'What about you, young man?' She noticed my badged cap on my knee and frisked the wad of tickets in my face. 'In the County, are you? You've not heard Madame Ellis-Roberts before, I expect?'

I did not care for oratorios. It was not that that made me shake my head. A look of cornering me gleamed in Miss Ceridwen's eye. She couldn't bear leaving the house without a sale. 'I don't like *Elijah*,' I said weakly.

'Is that the one where he goes up to Heaven in fire?' asked Watkin, stepping out of the tub and drying his legs with one hand. 'How's this old Madame going to manage that?' He winked at me.

'I said she's *not* singing in *Elijah*, by Mendelssohn, Part I.' Miss Ceridwen was vexed, but did not give up. 'She's in the Miscellaneous. There's no need to make jokes, Watkin.' She addressed me again. 'You are not musical? People buy tickets to support the chapel, all the same.... You can manage a shilling one, surely?' she added insultingly. One of the daughters craned her slightly goitered neck round from the sink; everybody looked, to see if I would be beaten down. 'A treat for you to hear Madame Ellis-Roberts the first time!' Miss Ceridwen persisted.

'A bladder of lard,' Mrs Evans said to me. 'I forgot to order a bladder of lard. Put it down, will you?' I took out my order book and wrote it in. A bladder of lard weighed about four pounds. I often wondered what was done with such large quantities of everything. Was it compensation for deprivation in bad times?

'Well,' Miss Ceridwen resumed attack, 'you don't like *Elijah* by Mendelssohn, but what about your father and mother?'

'They don't go to concerts.' I had made up my mind.

'The fact is,' Watkin said, putting a firelit golden leg into his trousers, 'there's too much bloody singing in this place. It's the opium of the people.' I remember he had been active in the riots of the long strike; he was the young man my father had concealed in our stable from chasing police.

85

Sinewy Mr Evans curbed his raw son, who had radish-coloured cheeks. 'It's not opium if you're born to it. Nobody in this family can sing, but no need to be conceited about it.' His own face had the greyish pallor of the lifelong collier.

'A person's got to be musical to sit in a hard pew for concerts lasting three hours and more,' the elder daughter supported me. With her sister, they dragged the tub into the backyard. A harsh autumnal wind blew in, and Watkin, still half naked, bawled to them to shut the door.

'Well, oratorios are better for us than drink.' Miss Ceridwen smacked the elastic band over the wad of tickets.

'Nobody here is a drunkard,' Mrs Evans said. Her son sat abstractedly fondling one of his pectorals, liking the fire-warmth on his torso.

'*Generally* I was talking. Opium was mentioned. *Elijah* by Mendelssohn is *not* opium. Neither is Madame Jane Ellis-Roberts. That's all.' Miss Ceridwen snapped her bag shut. But before she left I asked for a poster to stick on our shop window. She gave me one and went off at a trot.

The well-known mixed choir of her chapel could swing one off the earth in its choruses. I had heard it once or twice in the past. For concerts, the men sat on upper tiers of scaffolding erected below the grand pipe organ, their abnormal air of obedience lending them a saturnine mien. The women, ranged on the lower tiers, all looked swollen in readiness for any challenge, and, at the conductor's signal to rise to their feet, they were a concourse of dark swans mounting in ominous disturbance of the air. Above them, the male ranks stood poised more rigidly, even darker guardians of the empyrean spaces. Our chapels were too confined for the ensuing mighty harmonies, ears too miniature for such impassioned shatterings. The walls contracted closer on a dense audience stifling in best clothes, odour of mothballs, and sense of occasion. Our concerts stifled me.

'No talk about America tonight,' Mrs Evans remarked, piling damsons into a saucepan for jam. 'Miss Ceridwen can't be stopped when she starts about America.... Went there to visit her sister that emigrated,' she told me, dubious of this unusual enterprise. 'Bragging ever since, saying women are the top note over there.' Mrs Evans, rarely leaving her house, looked contented enough, her two men and two replica daughters about her in the firelit room, and her big order for victuals in my book. Women reigned supreme over the twenty-four hours in their dwellings. They were not to be put down; and their physical stamina, developed over the generations, was needed. Outside, the colliers trod their exclusive world, its main province the underground labyrinths, and pubs and clubs above almost as private.

'She ought to be a Suffragette,' Mr Evans said. His tone suggested there was only one thing worse.

The younger daughter lit the oil lamp. A large brass contraption with a green shade, it hung on pulleys from the ceiling; the Evans's did not want gas or the newer electric light installed. Their warm room grew into a glowing citadel of night security. Quiet Mr Evans left to go down to his club. His son, dressed now, returned from a visit to the rhubarb-fringed closet at the end of their uptilted back garden. The nook would have a stump of candle on the tiny window-ledge and was a favourite place for reading the weekly paper he brought back with him, Horatio Bottomley's *John Bull*, popular in the valley with many thinkers.

I picked up my satchel of money. Morfydd, the elder daughter, teased me about the cash-box I used to carry about everywhere when I was much younger, with the result that for a time I was nicknamed Cash-Box Davies by the boys of the elementary school. It took me a long time to live down. The black-and-gold tin box, its handle on the lid's centre, had been discarded in our shop; I kept crayons, foreign stamps and marbles in its beautifully-fitting trays. Early anxiety, rooted in guilt, had manifested itself in fear of loss of my beloved box. It went with me in the streets, to bed, and, once, to chapel. But people thought it foreshadowed an usurious future, with great respect for money, and, losing her shrewd judgement for once, the midwife had prophesied I would be a rich man.

Watkin came with me down the steep hill to the vale's flat reach of shops. He borrowed a Monday night couple of shillings; after all, he had supported me in rejection of *Elijah* tickets. He was curious about my school — very few sons of colliers went to the County then — and confided to me that he had once wanted to become a preacher. He was a member of the Marxian Club now. 'You ought to come and work in the pits,' he said suddenly, 'or the Kaiser will get you if the war's going on.' I was astonished, and flattered. It had never occurred to me that I might be destined for the pits or thought suitable for them. 'You could work with me down in Number 1,' Watkin said, no doubt at all of my suitability in his manner.

I had become more conscious of the colliers as a race apart, though, like most of them, I thought of their crusading battles as local strife with no schematic relation to the social upheavals (including the women's suffrage movement, about to be victorious) proceeding in the great world beyond our mountain ramparts. The sealed valley gave concentration to the men's struggles. The Cambrian Combine, largest and most profitable of our underground kingdom, still came under ceaseless attack. I listened regularly to a young agitator on a Tonypandy street corner on Saturday nights. He lashed slanderous abuse at named pit-owners and their general managers, including Sir Leonard Llewellyn, who lived half a mile distant in a high, tree-girt mansion which had been guarded by police and soldiers during the worst smoulderings in the twelve-month strikes which nobody forgot. For this hammering agitator nationalization of the coal industry was the panacea.

The race dwelt in the perpetual night of down-under and, day-shift or night-shift, sat in less sun than other men. Ghosts summoned from the underworld by Odysseus came to my mind when, one dawn, I saw night-shift men going home from the Clydach Vale pits. Returning from Easter days in Carmarthenshire, I had lost my train connexion in Cardiff and, its only passenger hours later, taken the milk and newspaper train up into our dark lumps of mountains. A convolvulus pink touched the craggy heights when I alighted at Tonypandy station and began to walk the steep mile to Clydach. All the place slept in deep lanes of silences. There was nobody but me to view the day's prim arrival. Then a clatter, sharp as the rapping of drums, came from the smudged greyness ahead on the hill. An anonymous tribe descended in clouting nailed boots from the slope's brow. Coming nearer, the black-faced cavalcade brought subterranean tangs into the new air; as I threaded through the pavement groups, eyeballs shone with marble whiteness in the unknown black-bull faces, wet red lips shone vivid. I would have recognized several of the men after their washing. Some greeted me by name. 'Been out helping to bring something down the spout, have you?' one of them shouted to me. My little bag was similar to the one for ever accompanying the midwife. The clattering faded away down the hill. There would be a climb into bed for long daytime hours of sleep, followed by a short while for above-ground events, and then the owlish crying of the colliery hooter would sound, and the tribe I saw in the dawn would vanish back into the earth.

I had good pocket money, took to cigarettes, chose my own shirts, and developed an impatience of the County school. If the war persisted I would be called up. I bought a pair of spats and a silver-topped malacca stick. These were not for school, but hopefully emblematic of freedom for my trips to Cardiff and the seaside town of Porthcawl. Backward though I was in many respects, with low terminal reports continuing, nevertheless cardinal developments seemed to be normal. At home it was decided I would be suitable presently for the sanctuary of Barclays Bank, and I offered no immediate resistance to this sensible plan. There was a shortage of labour and almost anybody could get a job.

I made a friend of an optimistic apprentice in a chemist's shop. John wore his dead father's gold watchchain and, a year older than me (in calendar time; more, in other respects), talked expertly of sex matters. He always carried in his waist-coat pocket a symbol of his maturity, calling it 'My Faith, Hope and Charity'. It was taken from the chemist's shop's stock, and he stole one for me, in exchange for a half a pound of rationed butter which I smuggled out of my father's shop. 'It's a funny thing,' he declared, handing me the little square envelope, 'but a French letter in my pocket helps me to concentrate when I'm studying hard at home for my dispenser's exam. Take my word for it, it'll do the same when you're sitting for those end-of-term ones in the County.' Among other educative items culled from his trade, he told me always to take permanganate of potash in my bag when I went on holiday.

Acute pessimism was apt to stalk his optimism sometimes. I did not hear that he ever turned his Faith, Hope and Charity to account. After church on Sundays, we walked up and down crowded Dunraven Street in Tonypandy, traditional place and time for pickings-up and sketchy wooings in shop doorways. Ballads of fiercely virginal girls tittered up and down in the wartime gloom, above which no Zeppelin was likely to sail. On the girls' heels squawked the noisy collier youths and a sprinkling of such as John and me. Sometimes we achieved a shop-doorway half-hour with two breathless girls; they'd bounce away squealing at John's daring sallies. He had, to me, an irritating habit of jingling coins in his trouser pocket and saying to a girl, 'You're a nice number'. Pessimism came to him usually on our forlorn Thursday evenings together, when few girls paraded Dunraven Street.

'Married women are best,' he confided. 'But you've got to be advanced to set about them. There's one comes in J.B.'s and looks at me you know how. She powders and keeps buying Phul Nana scent. The boss knows her. Comes from Swansea and her husband works in the powerhouse on nightshifts, an engineer or something, and she's got no babies yet.'

'You told me some women can't have them,' I said vaguely.

'All the better. This one's over thirty. I bet old J.B. thinks he'd like a sniff of her Phul Nana between the bubs himself. But she looks at *me* — likes them young, I expect. Next time, I'm going to tell her we can't get any more Phul Nana because of the war, but a chemist pal in Treherbert has got old stock and shall I take a bottle up one night after shop? Then we'll see. It all depends.'

'How?' I asked, half impressed by such an elaborate strategy.

'Whether she says a plain "Yes" or "No", you *twp*. When they're married they don't beat about the bush any more, like these chicken-hearted teasers we put up with in this street. They're straight.' Brooding, he fingered his father's watchchain as we sheltered from the black rain in a shop doorway, I leaning back on my silver-topped malacca stick and John on his ebony one. 'I think more and more about married women now,' he pursued. 'Coming into a chemist's, they *make* you think of the body. Nothing's a mystery to me any more, all the way up from bunions to hair shampoos.'

The ruse with the Swansea native did not succeed; John said that when he made his offer she bought another scent called California Poppy, and he took it for a definite 'No'. I was interested in a chemist's information, but John's ever-lasting cut-and-dried lasciviousness left me wary without my knowing it. He did not absorb me as had simple Jim Reilly and some other collier-family boys. But I was to find that, in one instance, he had been reasonably correct when he said married women were straight and didn't beat about the bush.

I went alone one August for a week's holiday at Porthcawl, staying at a small boarding-house kept by a former customer of my father who had gone to live there on account of her husband's silicosis chest. Flanked by soft golden sand-dunes on one side of the town, jagged piles of rocks on the other, the respectable place had always been my bucket-and-spade idea of paradise. There I had first smelled sweet-peas when my mother bought a bunch at a flower nursery, and for ever afterwards found the town in the scent of a single bloom. The air is invigorating in Porthcawl.

There, on the sixth day of this holiday on my own, I drank my first bottle of Bass ale, in the good-class bar of the Esplanade Hotel. It was my father's favourite ale and it made him cheerful. The barmaid had hesitated for a moment, to decide if I was of legal drinking age, but she gave me the benefit of the doubt. The hot weather had been tanning all the week. I had written poems at quiet Rest Bay, had visited the mysterious Edgar Allan Poe pools among the dank marram reeds at the long-ago drowned village of Kenfig, and also seen lonely old Sker House in which, according to legend, a daughter was kept chained to a wall after doing something or other typical of her savage day — R.D. Blackmore, author of *Lorna Doone*, had written an unreadable novel about the place. For my last night in stimulating Porthcawl the courage of drinking a first bottle of Bass seemed appropriate.

I sat on a plush wall-bench behind a table. Most people were standing. In Porthcawl women mixed with men in good-class bars. A woman sitting on my bench looked at me, at my Bass, at my smart malacca stick. She was alone, and, after a while, asked, 'Here on holiday?' Later she told me she had noticed me strolling on the front that week. She was on holiday too, from Cardiff. Her face was quiet, with nothing flighty in it to my eye.

I judged her to be about thirty. She was nattily dressed in a rose-pink blouse and grey silk gloves. A long narrow skirt was held by a waist belt which had a peculiar metal clasp of wrought silver. I admired the clasp. 'It's Egyptian,' she said. 'My husband bought it in Alexandria.' Married! I thought of John's remarks and gained confidence. She would not allow me to get her a drink. Hers was in a wine-glass with a cherry. I did not get another for myself; one was enough. Soon we left to take a stroll in the soft night air. She told me she believed in reincarnation, explained what it was, and said she could see people's auras. In the bar she had noticed that mine was blue, and I saw no reason to doubt her information that this betokened spirituality. By that time we had reached the sand-dunes fringing deserted Tresco Bay. It was well past ten o'clock, but the dark was a seaside dark, a blue spaciousness deepening to starry purple. I always had good eyesight and could see that her neck and a V-patch of chest-flesh were clean.

The sea lay afar, but was on the turn. Still talking of the fascinating reincarnation theory, we sat in a dip of the warm dunes. She suddenly kissed me. I thought of John again, and became him. We lay down. She treated it all as natural to a holiday. 'These hobble skirts!' she complained, clutching at the fashionable garment. She did not smile at my clumsiness, adjusting herself to it with what must have been patient experience. John was right.

For myself, clumsiness went and, for a short while, was replaced by something decisive belonging entirely to my own identity, unrelated to this woman. But months had passed since one night, tired of anxiety about it in my pocket, I had dropped the French letter John gave me into the letter-box of the Rhondda Urban Council offices in Pentre. The woman did not remove her grey silk gloves, and thereafter they always came first to my remembering mind. The business was quick and deficient of the imaginative pleasures of the Tonypandy talks with John. As soon as I rolled back on to the shifty sand I wanted to return to my boarding-house, though I did not have there the permanganate of potash John had advised.

The *ah … ahing* of the running tide sounded urgent. But my companion did not want to go. I had made the mistake of not getting to my feet. After easing her difficult skirt down from her hips, the woman lay back, held my hand tight, and talked. 'I knew you in Ancient Egypt,' she began, in a faraway voice. She spoke of bonds forged centuries ago. She had been attached to a temple as handmaiden to a priestess, was not sure yet of my capacity there, but had a crystal ball at home in Cardiff which she could consult. I listened politely. Accustomed to the religious flights of my race, I was ready enough to accept that the ancient bonds gave sanction to our meeting. But I wanted to get to the boarding-house and sort myself out. The experience was both big and small.

The sand was getting cold. My companion noticed my restlessness at last, sat up, and said she'd like to see me in Cardiff. 'My husband works in a coaler,' she said. 'He believes in reincarnation too. You could meet him next time his ship docks.' It surprised and reanimated me. She said she worked in R.E. Jones's Carlton restaurant in Queen Street and I could call for her there. I had already told her I was leaving the next day for the Rhondda, and dread came that she'd ask for my address now. She didn't. I promised to call at the Carlton, she told me her full name, and I said mine was John.

I did not want to dance over the dunes as we left. In the boarding-house I soapily washed myself twice. Other fears became entangled in guilt, with its rumblings of inescapable punishment. What if I had put her in the family way? There had been three or four such scandals in Clydach Vale, unmarried girls suing men in court. A young man living in Mortimer Street had been banished to New Zealand by his parents. It was some relief to remember — if she had told the truth — that my woman had a husband. *Had* I mentioned the part of the Rhondda where I lived? If she went to our police station could I be tracked down from description of me? It did not occur to me that I was not a 100 per cent culprit. Men were the ones on top. The event began to seem not worthwhile.

Back in the Rhondda, it was five days before I met John for our regular Thursday evening. In retrospect the event shone better, its reality altered. I wanted to boast. John listened, playing with his watchchain, then said, 'On Saturday, was it? Today is Thursday. Any signs yet?' And he gave information that disease showed itself in either three days or three weeks. So I had about a fortnight to wait. He spoke with righteous judgement. 'If she lived in Ancient Egypt she must be pretty long in the tooth. Married, my backside! I'd bet half a quid you'll find her doing Bute Street any night.' His lack of congratulation and respect added to my guilt and disappointment.

From then our friendship took a different turn. His academic information began to irritate me. He was the boaster, not I. And, as it turned out, his abuse of the Egyptian temple hand-maiden was unfair. I saw her once more. On my Saturday afternoon trips to Cardiff I avoided going near the Carlton, where I had often enjoyed the excellent plaice-and-chips teas, with a trio of piano, cello and violin under palm trees in the balconied main restaurant. The furies did not neglect me however. Winter had come when one afternoon in Cardiff I read a poster announcing a public lecture on Occultism to be given that evening at the premises of the Theosophical Society in Park Place. By then the episode in Porthcawl lay shut more or less safely in the distant past.

Fifty or sixty mature people already sat in a long, pleasant room when I arrived in it and, as was my practice in similar investigations, took a chair in a back row. A minute later, as the lady lecturer advanced down a centre aisle in an evening gown which had a gushingly long train of satin, I saw my Circe of Porthcawl sitting two rows ahead of me in a block of chairs opposite me. She had turned her head to watch the lecturer's rustling progress. An erect quill of bright green in her hat first caught my eye. In the hush before a chairman introduced the lecturer I cowered into reduced size on my chair, and glanced calculatingly at the door.

She seemed to be alone. I had an hour of indecision. I tried to pay attention to the lecture. It was disappointing — no revelations of occult tricks to be acquired, only uplifting thoughts about obscure powers latent in 'the vehicle of man' and brought to high service after long study and sacrifice. There was something called 'karma', an eternal load on the shoulders which seemed to me much the same as the burden our Rhondda Nonconformist chapels afflicted us with. I kept an eye on the green quill. It stood perfectly still all the time. Six months had elapsed since the Porthcawl night of nights; I had not entirely lost one of my fears, but I could not see my Circe's front portion. The lecturer sat down, there was hand-clapping, the chairman got up, and I crept out unnoticed.

The furies attacked me in the train home from Queen Street station. I had been worse than stupid. I was a coward. The sand-dunes episode took on glamour. She must have liked me. She wanted me to meet her husband. She went to lectures. She had a house out at Splott. What was I frightened of? A trap? I tried to comfort myself that she might have snubbed me at the high-toned Theosophy house. I belonged to a holiday slip. Surely she was a bit dotty, too, saying she'd known me in Egypt? I felt full of bad nerves as I alighted at raining Tonypandy with a group of half-envied, drunken, football-match young colliers, who bawled exuberantly as the familiar black engine hissed under the ugly bridge. This place wearied me. The trap was here.

I was surly when I arrived home. But in my overcoat pocket I had a thin book, bought that afternoon in Lear's arcade shop for no less than six shillings. After examining its illustrations in startled consternation I had left the shop, taken a walk, and returned to buy it. Random little bombs go off inside one with secret detonations. I took the book up to bed. It was an edition of *Salome* with the Beardsley drawings. Delight restored my nerves. I kept absorbing the drawings in my feather bed. The apes of Darwin's theory, which I had been reading about with approval that winter, were abolished and yet lay somewhere in these sinuous drawings of perverse yet truthful human beings. In the marvellous clarity of these lines civilization had both advanced without fuss far beyond its simian birth and retained the barbaric stigma. I felt it all in my bones rather than in my head.

This wicked Salome, in her Turkish drawers for the stomach dance, was more to my taste than the hobble-skirted dame of the sand-dunes and her reincarnation stuff. I read the text of the Oscar Wilde play and even I could tell that its illustrator, of whom I had never heard, made peculiar fun of it. I returned to the drawings. The alarming majesty of our Jehovah and other powerful biblical characters went awry and melted like wax. Of course I consummated the revelation, hot-house Salome and the concrete married woman of the dunes becoming muddled, with jealous John not far off.

Beardsley taught me that I couldn't draw. I gave up my dream of becoming a painter and stopped chalking heads on the coloured sheets of thick paper in which our raisins, currants and sultanas were packaged on Mondays. Poems were my compensation. Choosing Grecian subjects, far easier to contend with than anything under my eyes, I produced many dozens of Sapphics, entitling the whole *A Marble Bust*. I had already discovered heady Swinburne. The Apocalypse supplied a story for a one-act play, an ethereal *Judith and Holofernes*, swaying with lilac bunches of verse. I built myself a private lighthouse, went out less, became vain, and my uncle's unforgotten 'Only fools laugh' was forgiven.

School had become relentlessly dull, and my bad terminal reports meaningless. One day, a week before a new term began, I refused to go back. I had my way. My parents were very busy in their harassing shop. My father said, 'You're an enigma,' and I went to the dictionary for its exact meaning. He arranged an interview with his bank manager friend in Tonypandy, where there was an opening at the branch. The unconscious can produce a guardian angel when panic threatens. Passive resistance is the best sabotage weapon in its hand; in the long run, unlike raging or hysterical fights, it leaves few or no scars on all concerned. Throughout the interview with the benign manager I remained monosyllabic within my lighthouse and completely botched the simple arithmetical problem I was set.

'He doesn't think you are right for a bank,' my father announced at home, and my mother, like myself, agreed. She said, 'You must make up your mind.' I had, interiorly. I wanted to live in London. I wanted to starve and suffer — I did not lack money then — but the time for the experiment seemed not yet ripe, and I kept silent. For a long time I remained idle, save for the poems. The Kaiser's war had ended, so the expectation of my being called up had long gone.

My parents were puzzled by my proneness to writing, but considerately left me alone with this home-binding quirk which couldn't breed mischief. Would I like to work on *The Rhondda Leader? No.* My father learned at the Pen Rhys Golf Club that there would be an office vacancy in a Rhondda Urban Council department. *No.* But with the idea that I might be suitable in some capacity at the Cambrian (on the surface, not down in the pits), I welcomed an opportunity to be shown over the colliery on a Sunday, including a trip down-under. It was inquisitiveness.

No shift worked that day. But the great throbbing powerhouse was a breathing entity of shining force, unceasing as the mills of God, a heart of impervious machinery that yet generated a malevolence in its rhythm. I was given a safety lamp in the wonderfully clean lamp room. A long, streaking descent in an iron cage with an official, a friend of my father's, was invigorating. Then, beyond a whitewashed, electric-lit vestibule at the shaft-bottom, lay an eerie land of the dead, intolerably repetitious as passage followed twisting passage in endless blackness. We stooped through jagged apertures and trudged along dry tracks past heaps of broken rocks and empty rows of low iron trucks on rails. Veins of walled coal gleamed momentarily silver in our lamplight; I saw the imprint of an oakleaf clearly on one of these, a memory from past aeons of time. Timber-trunks propped up the weight of tremendous mountains. The scentless passages ramified for miles in this deposit of the third day. I saw no beetles or mice. There was nothing but the gigantic silence of unshifting death. It was not a hostile silence. Only the forgetfulness of death lay in this silver-ored beyond.

It was not a place for me. The colliery was another trap. Coal should have remained in its primitive burial, the earth's interior kept locked. It was a relief, on our return, to pat meek ponies blinking in their stables close to the shaft-bottom, a relief to find the pale autumn sky arched over the valley, fixed securely in living dimensions, sweet rain tucked away in its clouds. That evening I went to Cardiff for an orchestral concert, instead of going to church. In those days a porter stepped outside Tonypandy station when a train was signalled, and shook a large brass bell to warn laggards in Dunraven Street to hurry. I always liked its affirmative noise. It tolled for this hare.

Part Two

One: Twenties

I was my own interior master now. My feet trod the London streets without anxiety. The Twenties, in hindsight the sunset close of an era, were not a conclusion then. They coruscated with intimations of complete personal liberty. The animated metropolis thrived in a sociable attempt at demolition of class attitudes, the Labour Party was intellectually and morally acceptable, and Freud a newly canonized redeemer. It was a time to be young in; and also industrious. God had lost his formal terrors, and the Communists of the Thirties were in bud. Bounty, especially from the enfranchised women, was rife. Necessities were dirt cheap, and death at a halt. I never seemed to hear of anyone I knew dying. I was the right age for rose-tinted spectacles.

Eggs, poached and laid on the treat of professional toast, nourished at a kind cost. I ate dozens of them in those clattering, white-tiled chain-teashops that are no more. Close to the British Museum there was one of these sensible establishments where a cockney waitress named Olive would deliver messages for regular customers. This afternoon, after a matinée at the New Oxford Theatre at which I had seen Eleonora Duse in an Italian play, I had time to eat two eggs before proceeding to the Poetry Book-shop in a slummy street off Theobalds Road. Olive told me that my friend Anthony had been in, gone back to the Museum reading room, and would be at the Café Royal by ten. Aged twenty-one, and much more advanced than I, Anthony was trying his hand at writing a long, close study of the Elizabethan Age; of monied class, he was also an ambitious Bloomsbury Socialist and a member of the 1917 Club.

Duse, the only actress of the past I ever saw, had bemused me. She had come out of prolonged retirement to play Ibsen and one or two other dramatists. I understood scarcely a word of *Così Sia*, the play about a tormented mother for which I succeeded in getting a dress-circle seat after scraping together the high cost. Ignorance of the language did not really matter. The old woman went into a chink of my mind and stayed there for ever. Her moonlit voice, announcing hands, ashen wash of undyed hair and bony face bare of any make-up, worked the old anthropological magic. There were no fireworks. In those hands, displayed sparingly, a slowly dropped shawl took on the rhythm of a stave of liturgical plainsong. A lone pilgrim to a remote mountain shrine in her final scene, she dragged herself on her knees from the door to a statue of the Virgin, her whispered acceptance of death falling on us like quiet rain. Still in harness with these plays, she was to die an hotel death in America the following year.

A recital of poetry in a candlelit old loft, once an eighteenth-century goldbeater's workroom, would be in keeping with such a performance. I often went there for the weekly recitals. The loft stood beyond wooden stairs at the rear of Harold Monro's Georgian shop, in which the gaily decorated rhyme-sheets and chapbooks he published lay scattered among all the recent books of good verse. Admission to the recitals was sixpence. A religious air of repose filled the small dim loft. Windows were shrouded, ghostly chairs reached in the light of two or three candles. A shadowy man or woman would stand reading from a book illuminated by a green-shaded lamp. T.S. Eliot, who did not remove his close dark overcoat to read *Prufrock* and other poems, had been especially spectral, standing as if buttoned up against the damp souls of this world, and Edith Sitwell, tinkling out her early verse, had no look then of public-relations flamboyance or one-and-only mother of all poetry.

Even robust Anna Wickham, the reader this evening, lost her downright turbulence of manner in the loft. I had heard her reading before, and came to know her later. An Australian by upbringing, she was a great connubial tree of a woman, storm-shaken on an exposed hillside. This evening she read, among others, her heartfelt poem about a wild-blooded woman married to an unsuitable English gentleman. But her manner was particularly subdued this evening. After she laid her books down and there were a few handclaps she seemed to be apologizing for deficiencies when she told us, 'I saw Duse this afternoon'. Nobody replied. The broad squaw ravaged by turmoils, of which I knew nothing then, wanted to communicate with the small posse of orderly listeners in the dim candlelight. We shuffled out.

Two years now I have sat beneath a curse
And in a fury poured out frenzied verse.
Such verse as held no beauty and no good
And was at best new curious vermin-food.

My dog is rabid, and my cat is lean,
And not a pot in all this place is clean,
The locks have fallen from my hingeless doors,
And holes are in my credit and my floors.

There is no solace for me, but in sooth
To have said baldly certain ugly truths ....

Live women poets were new to me. Poets in Wales were always men. Awarded oak chairs and metal crowns (and cash prizes), they were robed and enthroned with due pomp in eisteddfods. Trumpets blew, a sword was unsheathed and sheathed above the chosen poet's head, while '*Is it peace*?' cried (in Welsh) the chief bard of the land, and '*Peace*' roared the admiring audience packed into a tremendous marquee. This dim loft was an English contrast.

When Anna Wickham was brought to my Maida Vale flat one night, after pub-closing time, I reminded her of her recital on the day we both had seen Duse fifteen or so years before. But her mind refused to fumble to the past. Battered, subject to sudden belligerence, wearing orange-ringed football stockings and be-draggled tweeds, she sat attempting to knit a hopelessly snarled garment from a ball of rainbow wool which kept running away from her under chairs. Wrath exploded in her when I mentioned the name of a novelist I had heard talking of her. 'Nobody who is a friend of that woman can be a friend of mine! She stole the man I should have married. Curse her, curse her.' This early beatnik poet survived, a tenacious ruin, until 1947. *Good Stabling for Poets* she had chalked on a board outside her chaotic Parliament Hill house. It was a refuge for homeless such. She hanged herself there one day, her body dangling from a window over her back garden.

On that fresh-cheeked evening of her recital I bought a rhymesheet on my way out, a Blake poem decorated by Lovat Fraser — '*Never seek to tell thy love ...*' — which for years hung pinned on the walls of my various bed-sitting rooms. I had a room in nearby Mecklenburgh Square just then; twenty-five shillings a week, including private-key use of the Square garden. This was one of my days off work; I was writing a novel. After my favourite gorgonzola cheese, biscuits and gas-ring coffee in my room, I went out for my street prowls, took a bitter in a low, corrupting pub I frequented, and, mounting from the Strand, halted when I heard a voice orating to a sizeable crowd gathered in the triangular space opposite the Garrick Theatre. My friend Anthony stood on a rostrum. I had not known this was one of his activities, and concealed myself in the crowd's fringe.

His cultured voice sent the Tories to perdition in the reddest Socialist terms. He thumped the rostrum with his fine pale manicured hands and earned respectful attention. He mentioned the long struggles of the Welsh miners, episodes of which I had told him, and I was back in the Rhondda again. Since coming to London from the truly democratic valley I had been very aware of that dread thing in English life, class-consciousness. In Bloomsbury and such haunts as the Café Royal this failing was kept under control, even if another kind of consciousness, intellectual superiority, was apt to show its bleak face here and there. Tailored Anthony, a well-born Home County and South of France boy, had never seen a miner, tended to be squeamish and rather grand when he forgot — or remembered — himself, but made valiant efforts to conform to a London, or Bloomsbury, Socialist uprising which had been established in the Rhondda and similar cradles long ago. Apart from this, and his attempt at a book on the Elizabethans, he read Proust in French, swallowed a wineglass of damp brown seeds twice a day, and, like John in the Rhondda, preferred women to be married. Listening to him spouting from the rostrum, I would not have predicted that in ripe time he would become an ambassador.

I went on to the Café Royal to wait for him. A coffee there cost a shilling, lager a little more, and a plate of the well-known game pie did not entail a subsequent begging for alms. Except for blithe Nina Hamnett, I knew nobody there. I still had my green youth to be rid of, and I had no valid right, inquisitiveness apart, to be drinking lager in the famous ground-floor room, then not re-novated. Nearly everybody there was some kind of veteran of the Kaiser's war, now almost forgotten. But years seemed to have been shorn away from the — to me — mellow women. Their twinkling legs acquired fresh value in curt jackets and skirts. It was extraordinary how they had rid themselves of the burden of old-style busts and a mass of domestic hair. Shingled or, less often, Eton-cropped, a negligent hand clasping the opening folds of an abbreviated coat, they trotted in and out with an accelerated pony gait.

Nancy Cunard sat at one of the marble-topped tables. She fed the eye more than any other of the women bohemians, her lovely head clarified by a sleek crop, her arms swarming with African wooden and ivory bangles. Her pioneering campaign for social recognition of Negroes had begun. When at last I met her, a few years before her death, those arms still rattled with the bangles, and spectral traces of the beauty remained. Thin as a rake, and tough as one, she maintained the Twenties tradition to her valiant last. On the day I met her, she had been mortally insulted by a magistrates' court fine of a mere five shillings, after a night spent in an East End police-station cell.

Nina Hamnett was another agile lady of the time, though then without the crane-legged thinness of her later days, when — a final tragedy for such a daily trotter — she broke a leg. She could hark back to the golden age of Montparnasse, before the war; there, to escape the attentions of the drunken Modigliani she had expertly scaled a street lamp-post. In 1912 she and Epstein had gone to Père-Lachaise cemetery and torn from the memorial stone on Oscar Wilde's grave a tarpaulin placed over it by the Paris authorities, following public outcry against Epstein's carving on a tombstone of every man's possession. Formerly a cherished pupil of Sickert, Nina still produced, despite her ceaseless goat-path prancings, wonderfully tranquil portraits, preferring aged women for subjects. Even Lytton Strachey, to her dismay, had laid an amorous hand on her; none the less, the drawing she made of him was one of her finest. Her own symmetrical figure had been sculpted by the poverty-stricken Gaudier-Brzeska from a piece of marble stolen from a tombstone mason's yard and, aptly named *Laughing Torso*, found a home in the Victoria and Albert Museum. She was kind to me. Governed by immediacy, she did not wait for any man to earn his medals.

I felt she had been able to prance from her mother's womb. When I first met her, in the Café Royal, she gave me out of her worn handbag one of the Bath Oliver biscuits she had dropped into it at a party the night before; at another time she fished prawns out. Like her friend Augustus John, she had been born in Tenby and invariably mustered up a nationalist sentiment for Wales. There was an occasion when she carried this esteem to the length of giving shelter on a bitter winter night to one of the revered Welsh Doges, a married academic visiting London for a solemn conference. But she neglected to lock the door of her hospitable studio in Fitzroy Street, and late in the morning a surprised visitor walked in before the drowsy pair could cover up. Worse was to follow. The water-tap had frozen. But Nina found that the W.C. flush hadn't and she obtained a saucepan of water for brewing the tea without which no Welshman can begin his day.

The London lack of concealment in everything intoxicated me. Oral revelations were lighthearted. If a love affair festered into lugubrious condition, a cold Freudian poultice was applied. It was not a time for tragedy, and there seemed to be no intimations of the blizzards to come; when the General Strike of 1926 arrived, it was a lark in London, boisterous undergraduates manning the buses, though in the 1917 Club, founded by Ramsay MacDonald and others, temperatures ran high in a different way. The family became one of life's chief villains, and the wedding ring lost lustre. I met my first — the first as far as I knew — Lesbian, a glowering and good novelist who, perhaps in mechanical service to her art, dived through a conventional wedding ring and emerged looking glummer than usual. Homosexuality — a term I did not know until I went to London — was not a thing to shut away. I knew, in the Twenties, only one man who took advantage of the new psycho-analysis treatment, plus a curative property apparently to be found in glandular injections, for his homosexuality. The result seemed unfortunate. Previously a normal talker, and of equable temperament, he developed a bad stammer and twitched like a marionette. But he married one of those patient martyrs who are always to be found.

My friend Anthony did not turn up at the Café Royal that night. Franz, a mutual friend, came in and said he was at the 1917 Club. Franz was the only really unhappy young man I knew. A deep and rank pessimism governed him. He occupied a room across the landing from mine in the Mecklenburgh Square house, and had taken me to the Café Royal for my first visit. A swarthy

German of Jewish ancestry, he was an ill-paid translator into English of Continental political articles, mostly Communist. I could not understand why he was so pessimistic, both in personal disposition and in regard to the world; but then, I knew nothing about Europe and little about the war. Aged twenty-six or so, he seemed to be a kind of refugee from Germany — an early herald. Because of his watchful jumpiness and other high-strung characteristics, I judged he had done something nefarious in his own country.

He achieved a hazardous feat in the Café Royal some months after my first visit there. One night we sat for a couple of hours over the single lagers we could afford. Franz knew only by sight a ringing-voiced Fleet Street woman journalist who sat at the next table in a grubby raincoat. We could hear all she said to her companions. She left the table to go upstairs to the telephone booth which, like a taxi-cab, is an essential of her calling. An old-style booth of stolid wood, with two small glass panels in its door, the Café Royal one stood on the first floor, close to the Ladies room. Franz followed the journalist without a hint to me of his intention. He entered the booth. He told me afterwards that not a word had been spoken, and, for the first time, I noticed the dark animal of his ancestral black forests. He had looked thunderstruck, too, when he returned to our table.

Just nemesis was to follow. The house telephone in Mecklenburgh Square rang for him one morning, about a week after his feat. The journalist, as is their wont, had ferreted his identity. She wanted to visit him that evening. Panic seized him. The jumpy refugee neurosis, or whatever it was, surfaced in whale size. The sleuth element in the phone call certainly seemed ominous. Could she get him turned out of England? Had he committed a public outrage even in a Café Royal phone box? Already aware of England's infantilism in sex matters, he panicked to the extent of suspecting some medieval law relating to the deflowering of virgins whatever their age. Beneath all this lay other fears. He asked me to be present for the woman's visit; we were to pretend I shared his bed-sitting room. He was in such a bad state that I consented.

The journalist arrived with a bulging paper satchel of German delicacies from Schmidt's in Charlotte Street, together with a bottle of hock. She was one of the new race of comradely women that had broken into Fleet Street. Square-faced, smokily hard of voice, and still in her dirty raincoat, she eyed me beadily but maintained a politeness. Once again, as with our servant at home and her poor collier, I became a chaperone. There was enough food for three. They talked of conditions in Germany, I kept my promise to Franz not to budge, and the journalist went off intelligently early. She had been clever in getting Franz to talk of his freelance work.

Save for that night, my silly chaperonage was useless. A bombardment of phone calls and telegrams ensued. Franz yielded to her summons to meetings outside. She found him journalistic commissions of a less left-wing kind than those of his badly-rewarded grind. There were Fleet Street lunches with her colleagues. Yet Franz's mysterious neurosis seemed to grow deeper tentacles. He took to going for sprints in athletic shorts on Hampstead Heath, running all the way there and back, and swallowing vinegar and grated raw beetroot on his sweaty arrival. His body was matted with black hair.

'Is it not extraordinary?' he whimpered, after yet another phone call. 'Not once have I made action again, not once. She is the descendant of the famous bulldog breed in English history, I must think. Is it the Ulster her coat is named? She is in it always. I think she sleeps in it. I do not know, no!'

She did not repeat her visit to the house. Franz, although he became better-off, clung to his cheap room. Then he went for one of those Home County Cottage week-ends which were such a pleasant feature of life and poetic output in the Georgian era. The journalist had a cottage and an influential Fleet Street figure for neighbour. Franz returned from Surrey engaged to be married. Furthermore, the British naturalization after which he hankered became more feasible; his fiancée knew how to set that in smooth motion. A kind woman, and a grateful one, she became a Mrs in her middle thirties, and Franz obtained naturalization and also a staff job on a newspaper. His wife was to part from him after two years. She gave herself an Eton crop and looked much younger in riddance of all else.

From a seat aloft, I saw them entering the stalls at the Russian Ballet one night shortly after their marriage. The journalist's awful raincoat had gone. During her wooing of Franz she had sometimes sent him complimentary tickets for theatres; he would take me, and I would remember Esther's poor collier and the Tonypandy Empire Theatre. I hadn't been invited to the wedding, or to the Bayswater flat the couple took. But Franz came to see me occasionally. He remarked once that he had a claustrophobic fear of phone boxes, but his obscure neurosis seemed to gnaw him less. His inability to smile remained, like his sombre forebodings of the future of Europe. But he had a Jewish dependability. When I had a novel accepted in London he made loyal, though vain, attempts to find a publisher for a translation of it he wanted to make for down-and-out Germany.

Nearly everybody I knew went to Diaghilev's Russian Ballet. I had first wandered into a theatre to see this astounding phenomenon shortly after arriving in London. The curtain rose on an item entitled *Contes russes*. Its eruption of barbarically primary colours gave much more than visual impact; colour shot down the throat, attacked the spine, poked up an erotic tumult. The dancers leapt with extraordinary abandon or stood flower-still with classic grace. Best of all was the last item, the balls-shaking *Prince Igor*, its warriors dancing as only Russians can dance those Polovtsian exuberances. Diaghilev gave his ballets a signature and triumphant dash I was not to see equalled, their predominant sensuality achieving a purity which reached the androgynous. They were a Slav fusion of robust flesh become colour and running lines of poetry. I kept feeding at the warlock's bounty for most of his regular London seasons in the Twenties. The fabled Nijinsky had gone into insanity, but I saw regal Karsavina in *Petrushka*, *Schéhérazade* and *The Good-Humoured Ladies*, and Massine and Lopokova romping in *La Boutique Fantasque* as nobody else ever romped, and, supreme of them all, the miraculous Spessivtseva as an Aurora beyond human jurisdiction. After dozens of visits I couldn't tell one technical dance step from another. One need not know the composition of planets, orchid-buds, comet-tails, leaping salmon, greyhounds. After life in the Rhondda Valley the heap of ballets I saw was a rainbow wash of the mind. They assisted at liberation.

Two: Eggcup Wealth

The Progressive Bookshop, a large, muddled cupboard situated in Red Lion Street, off Holborn, was the publishing address of *The New Coterie*, a magazine edited by a Czech poet, Paul Selver. Inside the shop there was room for four thin persons, three stout; other habitués talked on the pavement, in a pub across the road or in an adjacent pull-up-for-carmen café. The shop had a basement room in which, among corded packages of the magazines, a decrepit sofa was at the disposal of writers or allied human beings, of either sex, who might require a metropolitan night away from rustic commitments.

Charles Lahr, the shop's owner, had long since fled his native Germany. His attendant wife, a shrewd book-loving Jewess, cut through his rhetorical flightiness, sentimentalities and business generosities with the same realistic common sense that my mother possessed. She made cabbage soup in a nearby Dickensian house of this appropriate district, where Mrs Gamp had blown round the corner from her abode above the barber's. In the shop was a coming and going of post-Marx exiles from Central Europe and Russia; studious Jews argued, including an impressive melancholiac named Koteliansky, and freelance journalists and translators dropped in for obscure Socialist and Communist periodicals. Lahr was to get into trouble with the authorities later.

He also published one or two under-the-counter items for the officially disgraceful D.H. Lawrence, friend of Koteliansky. I couldn't afford to buy the Florence first edition of *Lady Chatterley's Lover* which Lahr offered me; but he lent it to me. I had just bought the costly Paris second edition of *Ulysses*. Despite the strict official ban, Joyce's book was not difficult to obtain in London if you were told where to go; my copy travelled by the Royal Mail from Birrell and Garnett's select bookshop in Gerrard Street, where Ramsay MacDonald's 1917 Club offset the atmosphere spread by perambulating Soho tarts outside. *Ulysses* floored me until it became a bore — 'Obscenity,' D.H. Lawrence dismissed it, when I met him in France later; 'cerebral obscenity'. The two novelist beacons of the English Twenties flared incompatibly. *Lady Chatterley's Lover* was too evangelically uxorious and humourless for me, but *Women in Love*, the first Lawrence book I read, had gone to my head and — the author's preferred objective — bowels.

The Progressive Bookshop became a port of call for me. There I met contributors to *The New Coterie*, the first writers I knew who did not want to do anything else. There was grim Liam O'Flaherty, Irish to his insurgent bones; the dreaming English country boy, H.E. Bates; the Jewishly ambitious Louis Golding; energetic Rupert Croft-Cooke of the roving eye; and Hugh MacDiarmid, on red excursions from one-and-only royal Scotland, and nautical James Hanley. The painter William Roberts brought in his striking cover designs for the magazine, and the shop lay on the extensive beat of Nina Hamnett, another contributor, as was the Negro-obsessed Nancy Cunard. I brought a Welsh leek into this bunch. Occasionally there were normal purchasers of books in the shop; and for needy writers Lahr could find collectors of their published manuscripts, including open-handed Sir Louis Sterling, head of the H.M.V. gramophone company.

I had sat down one wet Sunday afternoon in the lodgings I then had, and by the evening I had written three brief stories. They were as clear of fat as winter sparrows. In the metal-bound trunk I had brought from Wales lay several large bluepaper sugar bags full of my verses, including my interminable Sapphics, *A Marble Bust*, and even I knew that all these were as unsatisfactory as self-abuse. But I had ventured to send two London-written poems to a weekly, *The New Age*. They were impressions of the Russian Ballet, and they were printed together. Sight of them in print had filled me with queasiness. Poor prose can get by; poor verse never. I cast away thought of the poetic laurel wreath I had wanted.

My pencil galloped that rainy Sunday. I sent my three raw stories to *The New Coterie*, the quarterly magazine I had seen in shops in my West End wanderings; they were accepted, and I was asked to call at the Progressive Bookshop. More substantial, a new firm of publishers approached me after their publication and suggested I produced ten thousand words of a novel to show them. This done, I had a contract and fifty of the splendid pounds of those days. The publishers, a trio of idealistic young men down from Cambridge, called themselves Holden, and after a spell they were to find that idealism is not enough in publishing; they folded their dewy wings, though not before they had found me an American publisher, Harcourt Brace.

Where are the gallant 'little magazines' of yesteryear? Robust productions, always courageously losing money, nearly always cut down in the flower of their youth, but the casualty soon replaced by another sprightly bloom, they were many as daisies. *The New Coterie* lasted for six numbers. I ran my nose along my first printers' proof with the satisfaction that is beyond compare. My carnal little stories were long-trousered productions, a Welsh mining valley their background, family avarice and brutal sex their themes. For some reason I knew how to arrive at a full stop; and now that I lived two hundred miles distant from the Rhondda the valley took on a form as restrictive as an urn's. I also gave some flesh tints to Anglo-Welsh writing, of which there was none then except that of the savagely bleak Caradoc Evans.

I never forgot my second love. Short story writers are saints. Their revenue is not much of this earth. They work largely for love. While great poets continue to be born, all fiction-writing is unnecessary, but if the prosy activity cannot be dropped, then the short story approximates closer to poetry than the noisy and dense novel. Payment for my three stories, when I began to visit the Progressive Bookshop, was a complete set of Maupassant's work in about a dozen volumes. But I couldn't enjoy him. My god was Chekhov. I had bought with my spare cash the small green volumes of Constance Garnett's translations and seldom went anywhere without one in my pocket. The perfect machinery of Maupassant is well-hidden, but its grinding can be heard. There is no machinery in Chekhov, only natural leaves, a calyx, an opening bud.

I settled to earning my living by writing. Unknown young writers could dive into this in the Twenties without horror or dread; shoestring living needed very little money. I wished for no possessions and, since taking my leap over the mountains, I had learned in my initial year or two how to be alone. At first I had felt myself a foreigner in London, more *en rapport* with European exiles there than with English people. I found among the English an indulgent dismissal of Wales. It was a country where visitors climbed the Northern mountains or, getting wet, stood admiring those impressive arrangements of earth's furniture. The native language was a joke. Among the middle-class Socialists I met there was a degree of interest in the crusades of South Wales miners, and no knowledge of their domestic life. But nobody dreamt of taking a trip to those bitter and sweet parts. On the other hand, the well-brushed intellectuals were far more aware of the importance of the crusades than the miners themselves. Otherwise, the Welsh, like the Scottish and Irish, were expected to be idiosyncratic and, better still, amusing. In Wales there was a folk antic called the eisteddfod. Occasionally we had the investiture of our Prince. When I reached France I found this ignorance even more depressing. Once, when I mentioned in conversation that I was not English but came from Wales, there was a blank pause before realization dawned. 'Ah! ... le Prince de Galles!' Our nationalists had a long, educative struggle ahead.

A couple of Russians I met in London (one of them marooned on water) displayed more interest in Wales. I was introduced to Sasha, a young ship's doctor, in Lahr's bookshop. He took me on a visit to a Russian cargo vessel lying isolated almost in mid-Thames, somewhere below Tooley Street; the captain was barred from setting foot on English soil because of his political activities in Australia. We had barely set out from the bank in a rowing boat when the lowering summer sky broke into thunder and lightning. A deluge of rain thrashed down. My suit was soaked. For the first (and last) time I climbed a rope ladder dangling over a ship's side, a tricky operation. I sat in my shirt in Sasha's cabin with a vodka while he took my almost new suit of rough tweed to be dried.

He did not seem to think it odd that I should be taken to meet the captain in my shirt. Because the day was hot I wore no drawers either. But the impressively grave captain took no notice of his visitor's informal wear. Seated at a book-strewn table in his cabin, he looked like a scholarly bishop. His doctor gave him two or three books bought at Lahr's shop. The captain had the steadiest and most searching eyes I ever saw, spoke the purest English, and was Sasha's equal in unsmiling gravity. He wanted to hear of the economic battles of the Welsh miners — he had visited Cardiff and Barry docks in pre-war days — and listened attentively to my recollections of the riotous strikes. 'The Welsh miners are con-structive,' he remarked, and denounced orthodox religion as a

mischievous shackling power. He suggested I went to Russia in
the ship on their next voyage. Sasha took me to a saloon where a
large picture of Lenin hung askew; again there were no smiles
from the crew members there, nor on the stolid face of a stewardess
who brought us bowls of soup. Back in Sasha's cabin, my ruined
suit of heather wool was brought; placed on the boilers, it had
shrunk to a clownish size, and, tight in all parts, my descent of
the rope ladder to the bobbing rowing-boat was even more tricky
than the ascent.

I saw Sasha, who doted on American films, a few times after
that. But I did not go to Russia. I had no political interests. My
inclinations were more decadent; when I had assembled enough
money I wanted to go to the South of France for a few months.
But a couple of years after my meeting with the grave captain an
English acquaintance living in Moscow sent me a copy of a
Russian translation of my first novel, which he had noticed in a
shop. I knew nothing about it; foreign books could, and can, be
published in Russia without permission or payment. The high-
flown theme of my novel, entitled *The Withered Root*, was warfare
between religious spirit and carnal flesh, with spirit a heavy loser
in this Welsh instance. The captain would have approved the
theme, up to a point.

My metropolitan garden was not all fair. For a person of my
eggcup wealth the worst blight was lodgings. A time had come
when I had to look for an even cheaper room than my Mecklen-
burgh Square abode; and then I moved constantly. The period
tribe of landladies infesting inner London need a full chronicler.
Hangover from Victorian days, their Bloomsbury, Pimlico,
Bayswater and Maida Vale rooms had, unlike their tenants,
seldom been turned out. The griminess was not so much a matter
of London dirt as of constipations of aged furniture, plus — to
veil the tribal avarice — a moral righteousness these harpy land-
ladies exercised over their hapless victims, mostly young and from
the provinces. Their houses were crammed with filthy bamboo
furniture and ragged carpets; rusty gas-fires adjoined padlocked
coin-meters from which the landladies exacted a Shylock share
from the Gas Company. Such bed-sitting rooms seemed damp
from the tears of sad generations. The soulless slatterns of central
London (in the outer areas they were much less dehumanized)
who let these rooms were of advanced accomplishment in

bitchiness. Keyhole spies, they were also gifted with baleful secondsight and the ears of cats. Experts in bestowal of humiliation, they loured up from nether regions or a room next to the front door, and, by a single look, could plant cowering guilt in the fresh mind of a country boy or girl. Sometimes, according to their depraved notions, they were justified.

Their few male counterparts could be as dreadful. I paid rent for a few weeks to a man who, wearing an ill-fitting wig and a home-made kimono, had a nocturnal habit of standing in wait at a turn of his dark staircase and switching on the light as his astonished lodger mounted. Dominant lunacy of the whole tribe was suspicion of all lodgers' visitors, whatever the sex. But I was successful once in kindling a retaliatory guilt in a landlady. Giving sanctuary late one night — secretly, of course — to a hazy friend, my rickety bed collapsed under us, two of its legs dissolving and the wire underlay tearing from its frame. Rid of my friend without detection in the morning, I summoned the landlady to view the wreck. An abject apology followed sight of her wretched old bed, and by five o'clock that day an up-to-date divan was installed from Catesby's shop in nearby Tottenham Court Road.

There were exceptions. Queen of all my landladies was an aged ex-actress in whose Maida Vale house I retained a room, off and on, for years. Mrs Yule-Parrott had long put an Indian Army husband out of sight, kept a flat and a grand piano in Brighton for week-ends, and laid on golliwog mascara with such a lavish hand that I wondered how she could see to roll her marvellous pastry on Wednesdays, when invariably she presented me with a small fruit pie. She pretended to that respect for writers that actors and actresses, harps through which our melodies blow, can display without going so far as to read a book.

Prostitutes were a bane in Maida Vale, long a district for applicable music-hall jokes, but less a historic nook of Edwardian mistresses than neighbouring St John's Wood. 'I won't have them in my house,' Mrs Yule-Parrott declared. 'The ground landlords are the Church of England Commissioners and they could make my lease void after a prosecution. Soon as I find a girl smuggling a man in, out she goes.' Occasionally one of the several bawdy houses in the street was raided. In one which I witnessed, on returning home at midnight, four girls entered a Black Maria with great good-humour, each wearing a fur coat flung loosely over underwear; the last of these carried, mysteriously, a cushion of purple satin. But it was a wooden chest, rather like a schoolboy's tuck box, that interested me as it was borne from the house by a policeman. What could be in it? I asked Mrs Yule-Parrott in the morning; she said, 'Boots'.

Yet when a new girl tenant of hers, aged nineteen, was brought back one day in a police car she did not turn her out after listening to her tale. Decoyed into a Paddington dwelling by a couple of well-dressed men of foreign aspect, this sturdy, milky-eyed native of Londonderry was held prisoner for two days, had escaped by a trick and thought it expedient to relate her adventure to the nearest policeman. No prosecution ensued. 'Of course she enjoyed it all,' Mrs Yule-Parrott said to me. 'But I'm going to give her a chance and let her learn housework and sewing here. She's an Irish orphan and hasn't found her London legs yet.' The domestic redemption lasted some weeks; cheerful, except in her pale blue eyes, Moira whisked her feather brush about the staircase with gusto. Then one day she vanished, with her suitcase and the rosary hanging on her attic wall.

My queen of landladies had been dead for a year or so when one winter evening, carrying a bunch of flowers to an ailing friend living in a mews near Bayswater Road, I was accosted in the customary way of that district and time. 'Those for me, darling?' asked a figure, stepping from a wall-corner into the murky lamplight. There was a mutual scrutiny above the flowers. 'Well, bless my tits, it's you!' Moira giggled. 'How's our Mrs Yule-Parrott?' I told her. Moira shifted her white fur about as, wasting no more time on me, she prepared to trot off. 'Ah, I'm not surprised. She must have been eighty for a heck of a time. One of the best, poor old dear.'

Nineteen Taviton Street, off Gordon Square in Bloomsbury, was an apartment house in a different category, civilized and unique. Run on a communal basis, its tenants held a monthly council in the dining-room to resolve all domestic and financial points. A housekeeper provided meals on a non-profit basis. Rents were moderate, yet usually there was a quarterly profit, which was spent on a house party for a hundred or so guests. Roger Fry, of Omega workshop fame, had been one of the moving spirits in this idealistic venture; a long, painted table in the room a friend sublet to me while she went abroad was one of his hideously futuristic productions. In the domain of private morals the quality of mind in a tenant's head counted far more than obedience to English conventions. The atmosphere of Number 19 was excellent for frayed nerves. Political and social-reform workers were habitués, among them Hugh Gaitskell, his future already predicted, and the meditative girl he married, Dora Frost. Dora Russell, yearning over the young, was a sympathizer. Elsa Lanchester and Harold Scott, founders of the Cave of Harmony night-club, sometimes entertained the parties, during one of which a dead man was found by the housekeeper lying in the basement area outside her window. He had left an upper room to take some air on a balcony; and next day the appropriate newspapers were dark with hints of wild doings among Bloomsbury bohemians and so-called progressives.

'There's wonders!' an old collier I knew in the Rhondda used to exclaim at any event. A sense of youthful wonder remained, I think, untarnished in me. I liked the cynical, hard-cored Cockneys and the realistic London Jews, and I could establish quick contact with them; Cockneys seemed to me English only in an accidental way. In my East End haunts I felt easy in a sense of multitudinous races drawn from all the seas of the world and durable there in mixed breeding for centuries. The noctural mystery of the Thames as it swelled into full tide at Rotherhithe, and shadowy vessels slept lamplit at the banks or prowled up silently out of nowhere, brought a relaxed content. Here and there in London were close alcoves of the Welsh, highly exclusive and more obdurately Welsh than those at home. I was not one to cultivate them; I wanted educating in different spheres. In 1928 a sweet lump of money, deposited properly in a bank, enabled me to go to France. It had come from open-handed America, an advance sum for my novel. I intended staying in France for as long as it lasted, writing a second novel, disciplined against pleasure. I packed my trunk, which easily held everything I possessed, and left on an autumn day.

Three: Blue Coast

First glimpse of Paris unfailingly bestowed a larger sense of liberty. My initial Pernod, on the Dôme terrace at Montparnasse, brought the expected tail-wagging. Staying one night, on my way to Nice, I had booked a lush crimson room in a Rue des Blois hotel, across the Boulevard from the Dôme. Addresses and information had been given me by Eve Kirk, a painter girl I knew in London, and by Nina Hamnett, who told me to avoid at all costs the evil magician Aleister Crowley, then in Paris and a frequenter of the Dôme (his celebrated suit against her for libel was still to come). I was disappointed not to find him then or when I returned to Paris.

A seductive atmosphere of tolerance, easier than that of the Café Royal, lay on the Dôme terrace. I had not felt such relaxation before. Of the diminishing number of the famous who frequented the place by then, I saw only the model called Kiki. Her face dipped in brilliant green and mauve Lautrec make-up, she moved from table to table with a poised finish, a woman with no more to know, steady as an ancient statuary above the waist, a panther's prowl born from her proud hips. She struck hieratic poses by instinct. A young Swede at my table, who was in the timber trade, told me her name. Intoxicated Americans, mostly men, seemed to rule this roost with expatriate aggressiveness. The Swede took me to a restaurant opposite the Gare Montparnasse which afterwards I learned was a favourite of James Joyce. My first Paris meal did not destroy the culinary legend. I decided to spend a few weeks in Paris on my return from the South, if my money lasted.

The next day, yielding to self-discipline, I went to a *matinée classique* of *Andromaque* at the Comédie Française, and thereafter never lost a sentimental devotion to the majestic spouting in that establishment, especially the outpourings of Marie Bell in *Phèdre*. At night I ate a snack meal in the Gare de Lyon buffet and bought a straw head-cushion on the platform. Eight hours of third-class to Nice, on a hard wooden bench, cost about a pound. The luxuries of France could be enjoyed then for much less than the price of living in reasonable London. In central Nice, during the height of the fashionable winter season, I was to rent a well-furnished room, with use of an adjacent kitchen, for less than a pound a week. Eating in restaurants was a pomp at a disgracefully low price. The French still ate their economy, and their sacred gluttony brought out their finest courtesies.

Morning sight of Provence, from virgin eyes thick as syrup after the night's journey across France, brought the other nourishment. An arrangement of spare pines and rocks on myrtle-green hillocks hoarded aeons of sunlight; gnarled olives clawed at ochre earth below. The glimpse tore away out of my sight, returned with a different assembly of form and colour-values, vanished, returned. Soon, there was the sea! Chalk blue under the early sun, a racial address scrawled between the wrinkled red rocks of Frejus, there lay the Mediterranean!

I arrived in Nice in time to be bitten by the last mosquito lingering from the summer. I took a room overlooking a side garden in an hotel opposite the station, kept my window open all night, and in the morning a malign swelling on my face presently filled with juice like a bloated grape. A doctor avariciously overcharged me. Later, there was to be *la grippe*, venomous in its southern intensity, but short-lived. Otherwise, the pink of physical condition was the gift of that autumn, brief winter, and the divinity of early spring. The coast had entered the last lap of its unruined era by 1928. Nice was not a gigantic juke-box. With an effort of imagination, Queen Victoria might still have been expected up in the palmy groves of Cimiez, while Marie Bashkirtseff sat coughing over her journal in her home overlooking the Baie des Anges, and Chekhov recognized the white birthday-cake villas sheltered among camellia bushes and winter roses.

I picked up an efficient German idler in a bohemian meeting-place I had been told about in London, the Café de Paris (now no more) on the Avenue de la Victoire. Ernst had been spending his winters in Nice for years, mixing with the large colony of White Russians exiled there. He liked to be made use of and was unfailingly kind, though years later when he became a Storm-trooper he angrily abused me for writing, after a few weeks spent in his country, an impudent short story depicting the newish

Hitler youth movement there. Hygienic in all his habits, elegant and a monocle-wearer, his relentless contempt of the French race surprised me in Nice. When one day I found myself afflicted with pubic-hair 'crabs', did not know what those romance-deposits were, and consulted him, he declared that the whole depraved coast swarmed with the parasites. He lived on an income derived from family estates in Hamburg.

He soon found me a *chambre meublée* at a resident's price. Madame S, my landlady, was a native of some forty strong summers. She and her husband owned two floors of a corner building lying off the Rue de France and close to the Promenade. They occupied the lower floor. In my six months with her I never once penetrated her fastness or saw her husband. Neither had the much-travelled woman already established for a year in the main suite of rooms on my floor. Vaguely of British nationality, Mrs Cronin was a confirmed drug addict separated from her husband, of whom *she* never spoke. Her ménage consisted of a trained nurse and a precocious daughter of nine or ten who attended a nearby school. We shared the kitchen, which we only used for making breakfast coffee and afternoon tea. Mrs Cronin, an abstractedly beautiful woman, scarcely ever went out and thought the Promenade des Anglais a horror; Sister Beryl, a Lancashire woman, was almost as reclusive. They had their meals sent up from a restaurant a few doors away; costing about half a crown for three courses, *vin compris*, I sometimes joined them for evening meals, at which Mrs Cronin would wear some remarkably fine jewellery.

All seemed quiet and suitable for a writer at Madame S's. I kept to a fixed schedule of afternoon work. In the morning I went out to enjoy the peach sunshine, which occasionally vanished abruptly and left us shivering in alpine cold for a brief spell. I took lunch with Ernst, who knew all the most rewarding cheap restaurants. The Cronin ménage, living round the turn of my passage, kept to a schedule too. At three o'clock devoted Sister Beryl, who had nursed in several continents, gave Mrs Cronin her afternoon injection of heroin, and they then settled to water-colour painting together — 'our pics', Sister Beryl called them, and was not above trying to sell one of the florid daubs to me. Neither of them ever read a book. I failed dismally to ferret out their past.

Rosamund, Mrs Cronin's linguistic daughter, did not fit so well into my schedule. She arrived from her school at five o'clock and took to knocking on my door to have tea with me, sometimes bringing with her two slices of *millefeuille*, bought at a patisserie on her way home — a contribution which was to give me qualms after a time. Plaits hung down her back like shiny barley-sugar sticks. But the child-identity could whisk out of sight and another person flash into knowing prominence. She had lived always in hotels and lodgings, some in far places of the world, and could speak a little Chinese. Sister Beryl warned me that she was light-fingered and concealed coins in a surprising part of her person. She helped me translate a passage of *Andromaque* while I was trying, vainly, to improve my French. Now and again I took her for a walk on the Promenade at six, just before her mother had another injection and then bloomed handsomely for the evening.

A different upsetting of the afternoon peace came from my landlady, though this happened only once a week. Madame S had a lover and entertained him on Fridays for exactly one hour in the room next to mine. This unoccupied room was kept locked. I never saw into it in all my six months; a communicating door into my room was not only locked too, but its keyhole, I found, was stuffed. Unfailingly at three thirty, footsteps slouched up my marble-tiled passage, a key turned and, after a loud shutting of the door in the passage, re-turned in the lock. Activity began after a minute or so of deep silence. It was a choral ritual, clearly heard through the communicating door. It was also a revelation of the Gallic thoroughness which, like the native talent for forcing all usages out of a vegetable, extracts full value from the provisions of nature in men and women. Madame S's Friday hour brought to me a readjustment of my notions of conjugal fidelity and customs.

First, a light creaking sound came, a non-human wheezing, the voice of an entered old bed. The human threnody began soon afterwards. It was always the same, and astonishingly prolonged. Its basic gurgle was not unlike a pipe organ mounting, all stops out, to crescendo. An underswell of male growls, varied with snorts like nose-blowing, could be detected. Why had this pair to be so vocal? The threnody would descend to a long-drawn sibilance from Madame S which was more a Violetta death-sigh than a full Wagnerian baying. A blessed silence followed, sometimes broken by an unintelligible gruff male word or two. Then the whole performance began again, even more drawn-out for Act 2, especially the amazing gurgling. After another silence, and promptly at four-thirty, the key turned, turned again in the shut door, and a shuffle of footsteps retreated. I could go into the kitchen and make my tea.

Except to fiddle with commas, it was impossible for me to continue working during the performance. What was the man like? I couldn't visualize him at all. I always kept resolutely to my room for that hour. Madame S knew that I worked in the afternoons, and I felt she appreciated my remaining away from the passage and kitchen. In all my six months as her lodger I caught a glimpse of her lover only once. On that single occasion they stayed in the next room until well past four-thirty. I crept silently across the passage into the kitchen, and, returning to my room with teapot in hand, saw a hulkingly broad, middle-aged man emerge into the passage. Of market-porter aspect, he wore a short blue smock and baggy trousers. It seemed clear that Madame S liked simplicity. I wished I could have seen her husband. Mrs Cronin had told me he was a clerk in the municipal offices.

An excellent landlady, a doughty believer in beeswax, brushes, snowy bedlinen, Madame S briskly turned my room out every morning, and it shone. Every housewifely virtue was proclaimed in her starched, whale-boned, full person. I saw her choosing leeks one morning in the picturesque Old Town market; no limp leek would have got past her palpitatingly dark southern eyes. She had a strong tang of those formidable national figures that sit in the cash desks of restaurants, bars and shops, caged Mariannes who should be depicted on the superbly engraved banknotes of France.

'A subject for a short story,' Trigorin remarks to Nina in Chekhov's *The Seagull*, after his long lament on a writer's life, with its interminable mental notetaking: 'a young girl, such as you, has lived all her life beside a lake ...' I began to see almost everybody and everything as a potential subject for a story. It is one of the best ways to appreciate people, since everybody requires shape and pattern if response, to and from people, is to be fully rewarded. I tried not to be cold-blooded about this, however: the problem was to find the right seat for a detached view — not too far away, not too close. I did not find complete use for Madame S; only a smack or two of her for the novel I was writing.

'I think as much as you do,' Rosamund observed, always interested in the manuscripts on my table, 'but I wouldn't write it down.' Reading a page on another occasion, she said, 'Why is your girl crying? I don't like crying. I want to hit girls in the school if they cry. The nuns there don't cry, and men don't.' She greatly admired nuns; I felt she would become one. Her self-contained oval face hung chill as a snowdrop; and I also felt in her a basic loneliness which, of course unknown to herself, she had already mastered. Her mother and Sister Beryl were always glad when I took her for a walk.

She had priories of the mind which I could not fathom. There was no moping. Sometimes she tittered hysterically, or gave vent to crashes of derisive laughter. 'Well, *is* the masterpiece finished yet?' she asked, peeping round my door late one Saturday afternoon. 'Mamma says I must not bother you.' I took her for an ice-cream to a large café on the Place Masséna, where an orchestra played on the crowded terrace. She sat there with a lady's composure and was much admired by the watchful French-women, who had speculative glances for her escort. She left me to go down to the lavatory. I had dreaded this. Sister Beryl had told me that the problem child had more than once helped herself to the coins left in a saucer for the old woman attendant who might or might not be around these downstairs nooks in cafés. I gazed at Rosamund's face when she returned and sat, bolt upright, listening to the music with an expression of scorn. Had coins been placed in that very private money-box, as alleged by Sister Beryl? I went downstairs myself. No attendant was visible in the mixed-sexes lobby of the *lavabo*, and no coins lay in the saucer on a white-clothed table there.

'Should we go for a walk on the Promenade now?' Rosamund suggested, as soon as I returned. 'I have heard better music in Hong Kong.' I decided it was not prudent to walk the crowded Promenade — what if dropping coins rang on the stone flags? — and we went home through back streets. On Monday, after school, Rosamund came to my room with three slices of *mille-feuille*, instead of the usual two. I wondered if she had heard of Dick Turpin.

The lax air of that holiday coast was not the best for labour on sustained writing. But I slogged. Occasionally I took a day off and visited a tranquil carnation-smelling estate in the hills at the back of Nice. It was run for vegetarians and persons requiring spiritual repairs and meditation; a London friend of mine had arrived there with a limp and the residue of a black eye he had sustained in a Waterloo Road brawl. Or I took a bus to La Colle, a village lying on the road to Vence, where high-strung Liam O'Flaherty sat writing a novel under a fig tree in the garden of an inn, living there with his patient Irish wife. I would walk all the way back to Nice in the midnight purple.

Ernst had already taken me to the Nice municipal casino and showed me how to play, to my loss. But, alone at Monte Carlo one afternoon, I had my visitation from the god and won a, for me, substantial sum at roulette. In those days you could go most of the way from Nice to Monte Carlo by interlinking tramcars on the low coast road, at a cost of a few pence. The florid old casino, all dusty plush, chandeliers and religious hush, was beautiful to me. Very aged cocotte-like creatures, with strange scalp-growths of dyed seaweed for hair, sat calmly beyond locomotion at the afternoon tables, as if they had been born, earned their living, and become mummified before those spinning wheels which still linked them to the corporeal world. Their claws scuttled across the baize with sudden animation, and quickly withdrew into unbreakable carapaces. They belonged to the immortal sea outside.

I left while the going was good, and alighted from a tramcar somewhere near Beaulieu, deciding to walk the rest of the way to Nice in the warm magnolia light of late afternoon. I stretched under a sea-wall and went fast asleep. When I woke, a round bronze shield hung low over the authentically wine-dark sea of Homer. This sea was my cradle. I lay drowsing in the same awareness that had come on a cold winter night in Wales, the voice of a brook in my ears. Once more I knew we are always alone, and never bereft of identification with the endless past. Only the future was anonymous. Why should that be hostile? Safety could not be taken away. My grimy load of undeserved guilt seemed to have gone from my back. Its substitute of self-expression in writing, some of it impure, might always be as weighty, but this was of my own choosing, and it was a full wineskin on my back. I resumed my long walk without a care in the world, the future precarious, but my account in Barclays Bank on the Promenade des Anglais to be currently strengthened by my afternoon's winnings.

I stood helpful Ernst a dinner the next evening. Ernst was neurotic in a different way from Franz, my German co-lodger in Mecklenburgh Square, whose intellectual capacity could provide a degree of watchfulness over his manias and obsessions. Ernst, a sensitive fetcher and carrier, had not much brain. Romantic sentimentality could turn to rasping Prussian-like arrogance in him. His haughtiness to waiters annoyed me, and protest was in vain. Clean as a whistle, a daily sea-bather throughout the winter, he denounced the French as gross, greedy and avaricious and was particularly enraged that Nice sewers disgorged so close to the seashore. When my alarming crabs came, they filled him with righteous satisfaction; one would have thought the parasites had never contaminated Teutonic men and women in their own land. Monocle in eye, he examined my pubic hair and plucked one of the moribund spots from my skin with a nail-file. Telling me of their erotic significance and rapid egg-laying propensities, he held the flame of a match near the minute creature on a plate. It suddenly sprang into a dance, exquisite legs unfolding and wriggling in ecstasy. I felt a perverse fondness for this balletic creature left over from an equally lyrical night. Ernst went out to a chemist and returned with a jar of lurid ointment. Two days of vile anointings were needed to finish off the affectionate Nice pests.

A compatriot of his came under the lash. One morning he pointed out to me a beetle-browed man in shabby clothes slowly advancing up the Promenade des Anglais among an attendant bevy of young men. Save for their exhibitory raffishness, the retinue suggested an academy of disciples accompanying a black-hatted Hellenic philosopher to some shady grove for discussion of weighty matters. Their dilapidated leader had an air of donnish benignity; he reminded me a little of the mysterious glazier we called the Wandering Jew in the Rhondda. He was Magnus Hirschfeld, founder of the Berlin Institute of Sexology, to be ransacked in days to come by the Nazis. I had not heard of him. Ernst thought he was shameless, disgraceful, a blight on Germany. How could he go about in public with those louts?

A love of poetry and music somewhat redeemed amber-skinned Ernst. Reading Goethe, he sunbathed on a *plage* opposite the Negresco, out of which poor Isadora Duncan had sallied one day the previous year and been strangled by a flowing scarf caught in the wheel of her car. Ernst had seen a dance recital she gave at a Nice back-street hall the winter before and conveyed that she was painful to watch, an elephantine ghost panting in effort to find lost harmonies. He himself had not done a stroke of real work in his life; an income from his family estates was enough for his moderate needs. He was inflexibly queer, without making a song and dance about it, or allowing himself to be browbeaten by social criticism. He kept a pistol and, with this in hand one night, chased a threatening Corsican from his apartment and down the road of well-behaved villas. He found me a capable linguistic typist of modest charges. Rigidly class-conscious himself, he greatly admired the English nation; and he too had the inability to distinguish Wales from England which I had found so prevalent outside Wales. I produced my short lecture on this subject, which by now rang hackneyed in my ears from over-use, but Ernst couldn't understand such quibbling.

My novel began to drag, as is their way after a time. Novelists should be imprisoned, fairly comfortably, until their grind is completed. The azure and blond coast, with its beckoning drones, was a kingdom of Circe; there was an all-night bar near the railway station, rooms for short-time hire above it, which her swine would have recognized. But I worked; I had been reared in the hard Rhondda. I sat occupied with a kind of Welsh Emma Bovary. She was married to a self-satisfied draper and, in romantic mis-conception of a man, conceived a passion for a high-principled Socialist agitator who indignantly spurned her bourgeois advances. In the next room, Madame S's noisy Friday matinées continued to provide me with one or two deductions, though, having no knowledge of her husband or ménage on the lower floor, I couldn't judge if down there she was a better housewife for her weekly hour with her burly *coq au vin*.

It seemed faintly coincidental when, on a Friday late in November, she pushed an afternoon-delivery letter under my door before unlocking the next room — my letters went into her box in the entrance hall of the building, and she usually brought them up. This one was from the author of *Lady Chatterley's Lover*. I had not known he was staying in Bandol, along the coast. In even, clean handwriting, the script of a well-adjusted man, he wrote:

> Hotel Beau Rivage,
> Bandol, Var.
>
> Dear Rhys Davies,
>   Mr Lahr sent me your address. Would you care to come here and be my guest in this small and inexpensive hotel for a few days? Bandol is about 20 minutes on the Marseilles side of Toulon: 20 minutes from Toulon. My wife and I would both be pleased if you come. I'm not quite sure how long we shall stay here — but anyhow ten days.
>
> Sincerely, D.H. Lawrence.

He was to stay in Bandol all the winter, until we went together in March to Paris, where he wanted to find another publisher for the already notorious novel the crusader had recently inflicted on unready England from Florence. I arranged to go to Bandol the following week. Besides this exciting opportunity to meet the great man, I longed, after two months among the flotsam of Nice, to talk to someone authentically English. Such work of Lawrence's as I knew glowed with the true puritanism of England. His men and women moved out of the page and followed one from it. I especially admired the short stories of life in a mining place, *Odour of Chrysanthemums* and *Daughters of the Vicar*. And *Women in Love*, though it did not coruscate with diamond-clear meaning for me, had an ambience and freshened language aboundingly alive with a vehement, if rather gritty, affirmation that men and women must be reborn; with that novel he seemed to me to have struggled through from an old, slack, dying world.

In London I had imagined him a remote, inaccessible figure, brooding and isolated in his later esoteric rages and fumings, impatient of the European world, flying from it to places like Mexico and Australia. I had learned very little about him as a person, though I heard that during the war he and his German wife had been hounded from Cornwall by the authorities. He had become a legendary figure bathed in messianic thunderlight and crying aloud, sometimes incoherently, of the deceit, falseness and dangers of the apparently victorious after-war years. He was a kind of John the Baptist in a wilderness. And there he was fifty miles away in quiet Bandol, which I knew of only as a place where wretched Katherine Mansfield had sought ease for her lungs.

Four: The Bandol Phoenix

In the train I wondered what Lawrence would look like physically — in a second letter he said he would meet me at Bandol station. I had seen only one photograph of him, a youthful one. I found I thought of him as a big, sombre man with a vigorous beard, traces of his mining-family milieu in him. He would be rugged and a little rude. But though he was not big, sombre, or drastically masculine, I instantly recognized him in the crowd on the platform as I descended from the train. He was smiling, even gay, his high voice rippling and easy, an elusive touch of delicate attentiveness in his manner. He gave a first impression of classless aristocracy. There was also a physical frailty, a fugitive suggestion of hollowness somewhere (he was to die eighteen months later). He wore a faded blue blazer, wispy cotton trousers, floppy black hat, and did not look English.

Standing aloft on a rock outside the station fence, Mrs Lawrence, large, handsome and bright-plumaged, searched for us over the heads of the crowd. She too was gay and cheerful. It seemed something happy, even a joke, that I had arrived safely all the way from wicked Nice. In the hired car which they had brought my nervous excitement and twinges of fear fled. I was very glad I had come. Lawrence looked at me keenly with his bright, over-bright, eyes, and smiled. Frieda laughed and looked comfortably ample. Just then I did not feel I had approached the habitation of a man who fed on locusts and wild honey and lifted his voice against the world's failure.

This first note of simple gaiety was not to be maintained all the time. I, like everybody who came into contact with Lawrence, obtained a share of denunciation during this and subsequent stays in Bandol. But for that first hour or two all was charm and ease and purring. Bandol, in 1928 was not much more than a village, and the Beau Rivage Hotel drowsy and placidly-run. It was the hotel to which, years earlier, Katherine Mansfield took her nervous exhaustion and her, to me, moving *Journal*. The *patronne* told me the next day that I occupied her room — information that Lawrence, her erstwhile friend, dismissed as of no account. He said he did not even know she had stayed in the hotel; he also dismissed her stories as trivial. It was a large corner room with a sofa for siesta and a view of the lazy little harbour and front. The Lawrences occupied two small communicating rooms down the corridor. At this time he was typing out his *Pansies* verses and painting one or two of the water-colours that were soon to bring him additional trouble with the English authorities, especially a picture of naked youths playing a ball game on the beach.

His finely-shaped head had both delicacy and, unlike his body, rude strength. His hair and beard, of a ruddy brown, shone richly and, with his dark eyes, were keen with vitality; his hands were sensitively fine, beautiful in their constant movements, particularly when, brilliantly, he mimicked or described people he had known. These features suggested a delicacy that at last had been finely tempered from ages of plebeian male strength: a flower had arrived from good coarse earth. Above all he was vibrant with awareness of other people. To be with him was to feel a different and swifter beat within oneself. The stupid little behaviour of ordinary life, the little falsehoods, the little attitudes, rituals and poses, dropped away and one sat with him clear and truthful. But he could be irritating also, a smacking schoolmaster.

When I was alone with Frieda, that first day, I spoke of the admiration and respect of the younger people in London, how eagerly we looked to Lawrence for direction. 'You must tell him that,' she said quickly; 'it will please him so much. Because he feels *everybody* hates him in England.' I told Lawrence. He shook his head. I insisted. He was disbelieving. I became perplexed: didn't the man *want* admiration and disciples, I asked myself, unable to see just then that he had been so wounded by English attacks that his old cry of anguish, 'They are all against me,' had become a blindly violent mania. Thereupon Lawrence broke into such denunciation of the young that I was discomfited. Ah, why didn't they stand up and fight to make the world theirs, why didn't they smash, smash, smash? Why did they tolerate the impositions of the old world, the old taboos and the mongrel trashy contacts of the civilization they were forced into? The men did not know even how to handle a woman. They wanted to be treated as women themselves. And the women were lost, senseless, vicious

— but because men had failed them.

He rapped, 'All you young writers have *me* to thank for what freedom you enjoy, even as things are — for being able to say much that you couldn't even hint at before I appeared. It was *I* who set about smashing down the barriers.'

Yet his arrraignment of the young was not so wholehearted as his raging hatred of the generation that sat in tight but flabby ruling of England, the moneyed and governing classes. It was they who rotted the land. The young he blamed for allowing them to do it without protest. 'Kick,' he said, 'kick all the time, make them feel you know what they are. Because you *do* know, you're intelligent enough. The young know, they *know*, and yet they let be. It drives me to despair when I see them holding back, letting be. Because your chance is now; the world is all wobbling and wants a new direction.'

His voice, which became shrill as he was roused — and how easily he was roused to an extreme of intensity! — would finish in a sighing wail. He spoke of the way those elders of England had tried to curb him — how, indeed, they *had* curbed him. 'I know I'm in a cage,' he rapped. 'I know I'm like a monkey in a cage. But if someone puts a finger in my cage, I bite — and I bite hard.' Sometimes he reminded me of all I had learned of Dr William Price, the burning prophet and early socialist in nineteenth-century South Wales.

Lawrence, a collier's son, seemed to be no socialist — at least, not in a political sense. His old dream of a community of choice spirits living in some untarnished place (with, of course, himself as ordained leader) surely held the world's welfare at heart from a safe distance? He had, too, an intolerant repugnance of under-dogs, which could have been socialism gone sour. At the Bandol hotel there was a young Negro waiter. Lawrence took a deep dislike to this youth. It was so intense, and its object so innocently unaware of it, that I was amused. To see Lawrence's eyes gleam with watchful revulsion as the waiter laid a dish on the table seemed grotesque to me — why be so stirred over the young man? It was his hands Lawrence watched: thin, dusky, nervous hands laying very, very carefully a plate of *vol au vent* on the table. I watched too, as I had been bade.

'You saw his hands, how uncertain they were, no *feeling* in them! No feeling. It's quite sickening, he can't even place a plate down properly, he fumbles, hesitates, it's like a dead hand moving, every moment I expect to see the plate go to the floor.' And the denunciation came: 'All his movements are so *mental*, he doesn't trust to his blood, he's afraid. Look at him walking down the room, look at his legs, look how they hang together and cower, pushed forward only by his mind! Ugh!' And he ended with a hiss of absolute revulsion. It was true, as I looked at the waiter's legs, that they were rather soft and dejected-looking, clinging together as if for company as he took his short, gliding kind of steps down the room. Yes, his gait was vaguely unpleasant — that hesitating glide, as if practised, and the subjected look of the legs. There was little that was spontaneous about the youth, certainly. But this fierce antipathy!

Out of such vehemence came the element that keeps Lawrence's books alive: passion. It is an element that makes his work ride triumphantly over the years (Lady Chatterley on her stallion apart). He cares, and he goes into the blood. Better an excess of this passion than none at all.

There was an English maiden lady staying alone at the hotel, one of those respectable spinsters who were scattered over the South of France and Italy for long cheap seasons. This lady, Lawrence swore, would have liked to kill him. Her social advances had been ignored. And one evening he wouldn't deliver up to her the hotel copy of the *Daily Mail* as she hovered and twittered about for it in the lounge; he had whisked round to her, demanding, 'Do you *want* this paper? I'm reading it.' The lady had shrunk back, mumbling that, no, she did not want the paper. But he had seen murder in her. In his shrill way, he declared to me, 'She would have had me taken out and killed there and then.' The following morning — her room was next to his, not Frieda's — he insisted that through the wall waves of hate and murder had been arriving from her. I think he saw her as some sort of witch. On my next visit to Bandol, however, I was glad to find that he had made his peace with her. They met on the common ground of painting. She made pretty little water-colours of local scenes: Lawrence did his strident nudes. Frieda was malicious. 'One of Lorenzo's old maids,' she said, telling me he had a weakness for these English spinsters. Later, when we reached Paris, he took me to tea with another of them, a resident he had known for long; and that one told me that she thought Frieda very bad for him, an opinion I did not share.

He did not care for the French — 'a slippery and predatory nation'. Sex with them was all in the head — 'all *mental* fingering of sex, a dirty business'. On another occasion he lamented, 'Nowadays all pleasure takes place in people's heads. They don't *do* and live funny things any more, they've become much too mental and smart. The old England is gone and you've let her slip away. You young don't know what England could mean. It's all been broken up for you, disrupted. I'm glad I was born in my time. It's the sense of adventure that's gone. There wasn't all this ashy taste in the mouth. The fun is gone. That's what you haven't got.' Again and again he harped on the inertia of the young in not springing to save the real, beautiful England he knew. And because of his tuberculosis one couldn't reproach him with his own long absences from the soggy land. Besides, was he not protesting enough in his books?

I think he judged me prosaic and too rational. Enid Hilton, a mutual friend in London, had sent him my first novel and he found it 'weird'. But we had a mining-background link. He would ask me about my childhood in Wales, my reactions to the constrictions and religious bigotry of a Nonconformist upbringing. He kindled to my accounts of the social and economic struggles in the Rhondda. My miniature lecture on the difference between England and Wales was not needed, and, although he did not know Wales, I listened carefully to the following: 'What the Celts have to learn and cherish in themselves is that sense of mysterious magic that is born with them, the sense of mystery, the dark magic that comes with the night, especially when the moon is due, so that they start and quiver, seeing her rise over their hills, and get their magic into their blood. They want to keep that sense of the magic mystery of the world, a moony magic. That will shove all their chapel Nonconformity out of them.' It made me think again of our moonstruck pagan, Dr William Price.

I met with approval when I said I preferred *Women in Love* to his finest novel *Sons and Lovers* because it gave more to my generation. 'It's the old-fashioned lot that praise *Sons and Lovers*,' he agreed. But *Lady Chatterley* was really his beloved, and his bible, banner and trumpet. Frieda told me she thought *Sons and Lovers* an 'evil' book — 'because of that woman in it, his mother'. Lawrence said he had come to understand and respect his father much more than when he wrote the book. He grieved over the hostile portrait. His father was a piece of the old gay England that had gone.

I did not hear a good word for the few writers whose names I ventured to pronounce. The French 'mental fingering of sex' was applied to *Ulysses*. Chekhov, a volume of whose stories I had with me, came in for an impatient lash — 'A willy wet-leg. I can't stand his gutlessness.' *Madame Bovary*, another scripture for me, was drearily flat in line and shallow in psychology. Lawrence's talent for mimicry came into macabre play as he described Hugh Walpole — then widely praised and read — as a great pompous whale churning the literary seas, 'spouting water up for success'. Aldous Huxley, of whom he was fond as man and friend, did not escape — 'Aldous dearly loves a lord. A snob'. *Point Counter Point*, which I had just read and in which Huxley vividly depicts Lawrence in the character of Rampion, was dismissed as 'Michael Arlen stuff'. Such blasphemy as that about Chekhov apart, I felt he could unfailingly detect the 'smart' in writing, the vogue millinery and cosmetics of literary fashion, its stylish and favoured wearers the real provincials, however metropolitan their reputations. I also felt that no writer could belong less to the literary life than he; he made London seem far away.

Perhaps he knew that in my room I was tucking a lot of this away; he had perception enough. I enjoyed myself, as a visitor. Lawrence seemed to want a good listener, he never begrudged talking, and it was impossible for one's attention to wander. When I referred again to Katherine Mansfield he gave a half-willing salutation to her as a person. It was her husband, Middleton Murry, who stood beyond Laurentian forgiveness. Murry's Judas kiss at the famous Café Royal Last Supper ('I love you, Lorenzo, but I won't promise not to betray you,') was not referred to. But in London I had read an account by Murry of his visit to the Gurdjieff Institute at Fontainebleau, where he had gone post-haste on hearing of his wife's serious condition. It was a moving and emotional recital of a last peaceful reunion, all past differences forgiven and resolved. Lawrence did not know of this published account. He listened to my recounting of it. He squirmed, he yelped. 'Wrong! *Wrong!* This is what really happened. When Murry turned up at that crank's institute a friend staying there went to Katherine's room to tell her of his arrival. She said, "Keep that bugger away from me," then had her last haemorrhage.' He did not reveal his source of this.

He and Frieda would come after lunch for rest and gossip in my spacious room, which had been Katherine's. Once he brought a sheaf of his newest *Pansies* and, not a good reader, read them in a stringy reciting voice, half chirp, half hollow throb; on this occasion I fell asleep on the sofa, which amused him, but not Frieda. He found immense fun in writing these satirical verses — or 'squibs' as he called them — composing them in bed in the mornings, a bead-fringed African skullcap on his head — 'It keeps my brain warm,' he said, and bought me one of these straw caps in a Bandol shop. The light-hearted, if barbed, *Pansies* seemed characteristic of one part of him. When I mentioned that this title might be misunderstood in England — he did not know its slang use — he enjoyed the joke all the more. He little suspected the ludicrous, heavy-handed official interference these little lizard poems were about to endure, though in the end they emerged triumphant, tails gaily up.

Crotchety in a schoolmasterish way though he was at times, he seldom irritated me. His personality came through with a full glow, often martially, but oftener in the eagerly bright recognition of other people's natures which was another prominent characteristic of his. He was a giver-out. He made me realize how tightly most people remain in their skins, their little glances darting and quickly scampering back to secret places. In spite of frequent mental doubt of his beliefs, elsewhere in one's being there was a feeling that in some ardent sphere beyond cerebral logic he was supremely right — there, in the instinctual self, was a truth that lived in him uncensored. I too received his oft-repeated injunction: 'When you have to come to a decision, whatever your mental calculations tell you, go by what you feel here' — and with a quick, intent gesture he placed his hands low over his belly — 'go by that, by what you feel deep in you'. When we reached Paris, the belly-message was to tell him to refuse a substantial sum of money offered by a conscience-smitten publisher who had brought out a pirated edition of *Lady Chatterley*; I admired, but wondered if I would have let the message go hang for once.

Observing him strolling about in the afternoon sunshine of the *plage* below the hotel terrace, I mused over his extraordinary attraction as a person to look at. There was something of both a bird and a lizard about him — light and winging, no flesh hampering him. Yet the dark torrent of hatreds and teeming awareness in that frail figure! The curious bearded man on the *plage* was somehow electrically dangerous; he bore a high voltage of life. His irascibility had the crackling temper of a fire. He could devour even over such a trivial incident as being half an hour late for the hotel lunch. One morning I ran into Frieda on the *plage* and we dawdled in a café over aperitifs. Unaware that we were late, we ambled back to the hotel. Suddenly I noticed a dark figure watching our approach from the top of a flight of steps to the terrace. It stood poised as if for a hawk's swoop. As we mounted the steps, Lawrence's legs danced in full fury. A flood of highly personal abuse poured on us, most of it connected with bad breeding. Frieda strode past him, regally oblivious; I decided that before such vituperation a polite apology would be fatuous. Quite soon, the tornado subsided into a vexed silence, out of which came a charming offer. In the centre of the dining-room stood a tray of locally-caught lobsters. These were a supplement on the table d'hôte price. Lawrence, the host, was sure I would like a lobster. I shook my head; he insisted; I refused to be wooed with the bristling creatures. Frieda was not so foolish. She enjoyed the treat with an unruffled air of however extraordinary one's husband one does not have lobsters every day.

Despite the sales of high-priced *Lady Chatterley*, this historic pair were still not well-off. There were no extravagances of living. I could well perceive that in their yet poorer days Frieda had been a tower of strength to her husband. Their marriage seemed to me, on my late acquaintance with it, a prosperous one. It had not descended into apathy. Frieda possessed a lioness quality that could meet his outbursts with a fine swing and dash. When really stung, she would shake her mane and growl; sometimes she charged. Her spirit was direct and generous, and his could be laughing, malicious and subtle. Their notorious brawls — at.least, the ones I witnessed — were opulent. She would lash out, and, gathering his forces with ease, he met her like a confident warrior. He would attack her for smoking too many cigarettes, having her hair bobbed, taking a wrong line of thought, eating too many cakes in a Toulon café, or for attempting to be intellectual or aristocratic. He kept her simmering. A natural inclination to a stout German placidity could easily have swamped her fine lioness quality.

He had struck an aggressive note against her on my first evening with them at Bandol. It startled me. At dinner in the full hotel restaurant he threatened to slap Frieda's face across the soup. He declared she had got herself into a 'mystical' state through reading a German book on Rasputin. He drew a mocking picture of women prostrate and fawning around the dirty scoundrel, their faces gaping up for sensual religious sustenance — 'anything that has no vulgar body!' he jeered. It was true that Frieda, talking of the book at the table, had displayed a rapt interest in the monk. On this occasion too, in a decorous dining-room, I heard for the first time in my life a husband use publicly to his wife the conjugal four-letter word that has since carried *Lady Chatterley* into so many well-run homes. I cast an eye over the neighbouring tables. There were several English people around.

Frieda was not a woman to exercise female bossiness. She could leave her lord alone and keep cheerfully alive in her own being; she knew how to leave a man alone. Sometimes she seemed to view herself as an Athena; she told me later that it was she who had 'fished' *Death of A Hero* out of bruised Richard Aldington. But there was no bluestocking nuisance. To me much of her seemed to be a creation of Lawrence, her most successful validity as an alive being deriving from his work on her both in her everyday self and as the handsome woman in some of his novels and poems. She was Eve; and he that other one freshly gleaming from the hand of the Almighty.

In my first visit to Bandol he was blissfully unaware that our Home Secretary, Sir William Joynson-Hicks, was keeping an eye on the maniacal Bandol Adam; *Lady Chatterley* was not to be forgiven. But between this and my next visit news arrived that a typed collection of the *Pansies*, dispatched to London from Bandol, had been seized in the post by the English authorities. There was nothing in this incomplete set of the poems, or in later additional ones, that could be construed as indecent by a normal person; there were merely some bits of plain speaking in good household English. The authorities clung to the first collection, however. I dispatched from Nice post office a duplicate set, still incomplete, and this arrived in London without molestation, and later, when I returned to London, my trunk contained a complete set.

Lawrence, sick in the face, crying out in his bedroom of the seizing of his darling innocent poems, or raging on the beach as he talked of it, was depressing to see. He could *not* understand this new, mealy-mouthed England. How the old robust England of strong guts and tongues had died! Why, why couldn't they let him have his say? The charge of indecency had an effect on him like vomiting. It was painful to look at him. The 'grey men' were at his heels. In such moments as these I felt that, more than the tuberculosis (which he tended to ignore — 'my troublesome bronchials'), an evil destructive force was successfully attacking him. Frieda was at her best in such crises, a rock. One could understand her loving-wife remark in her memoirs after his death — 'Lawrence was the last green leaf on the English tree'. To me, this exiled man seemed to be more passionately identified with England than anyone I had known, an infuriated guardian of the nation's ancient merits.

The Home Secretary continued to sit on his sheaf of *Pansies*; and, in a year or so, a dozen of the author's paintings were to be snatched out of a London art gallery by policemen. Meanwhile, in tranquil Bandol Lawrence simmered down and added fresh blooms to the *Pansies*. The days were sunnily mild just then. Once or twice we took afternoon drives into the countryside in a droshky. Lawrence disliked motor-cars. While the elderly nag munched herbage, and Frieda and I strolled in search of the first anemones, he would sit on his heels and, eyelids lapsed from the sun, remain meditating like an old bird; I had seen Welsh colliers sit in that fashion against the sunny corner wall of Evans the Butcher's shop. But I imagined a Black Maria appearing and sweeping up this villainous fowl, the scraggy nag gazing around at the spectacle in astonishment.

There were other endearing characteristics. When I became afflicted with Travellers' Blight and stayed in my room for a morning, Lawrence, on hearing from the chambermaid that I was incommoded, appeared with an aged little Gladstone bag. Within this bag — I was to view it with dismay in Paris — lay a collection of those small narrow bottles and tiny round boxes of homely medicines which used to be sold in English village shops along with packets of flower-seeds and children's sweets. He dosed me with something dark; it might have been Dr Collis Browne's Chlorodyne. Equally soothing, he sat for an hour talking with extraordinarily funny mimicry of a lively terrier he had kept in

Italy which, despite a terrible prediliction to misfortune, refused to die.

The typescript of *Pansies* in my own bag, I returned to Nice from this second visit with even more admiration of him. It was almost as much a pleasure to leave Bandol as to arrive there. Lawrence was too absorbing. Within the charm and vitality lay a seductive despotism. He was too high-pitched; for all the sensitivity and outgiving awareness of other people, an impression — inaccurate though it was — would come of living within sound of a continuous shriek of agony. His former dream of a community of fellow-spirits dwelling in an untarnished place could not have found fulfilment, precisely because it was his idea; the men would have disputed his leadership, the women quarrelled among themselves for his attentions. He could grate on one in a way that wasn't trivial.

Yet all the way back to Nice in the slow omnibus train, third class, I would think of him and remember the strange vividness he brought to everyday events and talk. I also sought for blemishes. One idiosyncrasy of his became tedious: an insistence on a belligerent kind of masculinity was a foible apt to display itself gratuitously at any moment. Surely, I thought, one took a hairy-chest quality in a man for granted — or not, if it just wasn't there. A forced he-manship was tiresome. Was Lawrence over-aware of the element of feminine sensibility he possessed so definitely (and which was so valuable to him as a novelist)? And did he, perhaps from some puritanic standpoint, watch its temperature graph neurotically? It was his depiction of masculinity in his novels and stories, especially those with a coal-mining background, that had led me to expect, naïvely, a tough, louring person waiting for me on Bandol station; instead I had found someone fine-grained, a light-footed man of high-bred quality, a man clear of class-consciousness and other preposterous blockages to esteem and understanding. Patience was needed for his foible. The same schoolyard insistence on masculinity mars some of the work of Ernest Hemingway. Men novelists cannot afford to be 100 per cent male — any more than, according to experienced Somerset Maugham, they can afford to be gentlemen. (Did Maupassant go too far when he compared novelists to rats in a granary?)

There he sat at Bandol, ensconced in a nest of flames like his phoenix emblem, and if Sir William Joynson-Hicks poked a stick into the nest it only roused the immortal bird to British squawks of protest. I posted his simple *Pansies* to London as soon as I arrived in Nice, and when we went to Paris in March he was soon to find a publisher for a cheap, widely-read edition of *Lady Chatterley*. His seized paintings too, after a deal of unpleasantness, were to be returned to him. Virtue sometimes triumphs, at a price.

Five: Indulgent Gods

I spent a first Christmas away from Wales. By that time I wore a beret and espadrilles and took a Pernod every morning on the Place Masséna. I worked harder at my novel, and in the silent watches of more than one night knew that it was bad. It was the sizeable thorn on my winter rose. But physically I was on top of the world, and also rather sullied morally, for both of which I was grateful to the indulgent gods.

My preference for the company of people older than myself did not abate; it was as though I wanted to catch up thus on inner deficiencies and lack. In Nice I associated, except for nine-year-old Rosamund, with men and women who then seemed to me advanced well into middle-age. I picked up with a resident Englishwoman who lived in my street and worked in a bank. On Sundays she went to ski at La Colmiane, returning for a late cognac in my room so shiny with clamant vigour that I judged the sport too unsettling for single women. With her and her woman friend I went to one or two dances at the Municipal Casino and saw the sensible gigolo system in operation ('French fingering of sex,' Lawrence would have called it). Men of exquisite manners, but all of them melancholy of visage, the gigolos' attentions were courtly to any woman needing succour, and there was a spare one at our table.

Ernst took me to a formal White Russian party on one of their feast days. The head of the Nice colony, a bemedalled aristocrat, received the guests with regal friendliness. Most of these high-ranking Russians were poverty-stricken, some of them working at menial jobs in the big hotels. But they over-flowed with warmth and garrulity and had nothing of the grave, watchful solemnity I had found in the Red ship on the Thames. It was as though misfortune and exile brought a compensatory exuberance. A hotel kitchen-hand and his wife afterwards entertained me to supper in their blowzy apartment; there was little to drink, masses of food, perhaps snitched from the hotel, and abundance of high spirits. Nice was certainly a town in which to be poor. I felt rich there myself.

I had become a resident. Just before Christmas, Madame S, my landlady, demonstrated a kindly aspect of her cut-and-dried French efficiency. She came into the men's clothes department of the Galeries Lafayette while I was distracted by attempts to cope with a woman assistant who seemed determined that this foreigner should not obtain a dressing-gown on display in the store window. Other gowns, of the wrong colour and prices, were produced. I intended to send a dressing-gown to Lawrence, since he did not possess one at Bandol. Madame S, quickly perceiving that her tenant was at the mercy of the sly saleswoman with his elementary French, swooped. A hail of sharp Nice *patois* was exchanged with her fellow-townswoman. Black eyes flashing, Madame S cast gowns aside with a vindictive intensity after feeling their textures; bosom heaving, she spat words out with a glottal roll that made me think of her Friday noises in the room next to mine. I managed to tell her I wanted a gown on show in the window. 'Ha!' She grasped the situation instantly.

The gown was fetched from the window by the display manager. I tried it on and, as I had thought, it was the right size and colour for Lawrence. There was a flourish of compliments from the two ladies, now united in satisfaction, the disagreeable saleswoman beaming like an after-the-ceremony bride. But outside the store I made a mistake. I suggested to Madame S a morning aperitif on the nearby Place Masséna. An expression of deprecating rebuke passed across her face; there was a perceptible drawing-up of her frontage. I felt that her refusal implied that a respectable married Frenchwoman did not sit in a public place drinking with a young man acquaintance. She bid me *au revoir*. It was not a Friday, either.

After Christmas my friend and contemporary, Anthony, arrived from London for a fortnight. We went for a three-day tramp into the lonely frontier reaches of Italy, towards Tende. It was my first, and last, experience of such purgatory. Anthony knew the ropes; we had knapsacks, maps, socks, plain chocolate and cognac. Climbing north-west, after a long bus ride out of Nice, soon the morning warmth of the coast belonged to another continent. It was the short dead season of midwinter. The rocky earth up there smelled of frost and iron.

I had been reared among mountains, had wanted to escape
them, and could not feel their mystery any more. We could see
the distant Maritime Alps on our left. The bluish-white of their
slopes reminded me of the faces of the Welsh corpses I used to
view with Jim Reilly. Any Alps are lowering to the human spirit.
They are hostile to man. They do not relax. Nobody should climb
them, nobody stay up on those euthanasian heights. I plodded on
among stones and hard-tufted greenery. Anthony had long legs
and upper middle class morality; I, shorter legs and a lessened
load of guilt. But Anthony wanted to shuffle something off too;
the heights were redemptive for him. He talked of socialism and
his book on the Elizabethan Age. He was weighed down by a
brilliant twin sister, still absorbed in Proust, and had no use for
D.H. Lawrence's work. I remembered his successful haranguing
of a crowd outside the Garrick Theatre. But he was not a
chatterbox.

The air was wonderful and very cold. By afternoon there were
no human habitations and no birds. There was a hooded crucifix
beside an elementary path among great lumps of rocky earth. Yet
the silence did not oppress. Silence is almost a lost treasure. A
whole week without speaking to anyone should be spent by
everybody at intervals; but not among desolate mountains, which
bring madness without the lunacy. We climbed and climbed.
Save for the smell of rare air and the silence I could see little point
in the climb, symbolic or realistic. I was greedy for human beings
still; not necessarily to talk with them; the mysterious quiet ones
nourished me most.

'We're spending the night down there.' Rounding a craggy
spur, Anthony pointed to a close-packed village far below. In the
light of early dusk it had the colours of goats and the tumbling
grey water of its hump-bridged stream. We descended a wild,
rock-strewn slope. Soon my air-clarified eyes detected two sombre
figures watching our progress. Cloaked and feather-helmeted,
guns slung on their shoulders, they stood outside a cabin beyond
the bridge. 'They think we're fugitives,' Anthony said. 'It's Italy
over there.'

Italy was colder than the air in the mountains. The body-heat
engendered in the heights began to ebb as we crossed the bridge
over the jagged, deep-looking stream. The two men barred our
way. One held a fold of cloak over his mouth like a villain lurking

behind arras on the stage. They eyed us, professionally intimidating. Neither of us could speak Italian. We produced our passports. But we were hauled off by one of the officers to a building in the village. A cantankerous man in ordinary garb turned out our knapsacks, frisked our persons, peered disbelievingly from our passport photographs to us. He spoke French, questioned our motives in walking the mountains, asked me my grandmother's maiden name, muttered long and puzzledly over the mysterious Welsh name of my birthplace, and also over Anthony's and my own stated profession of writers. The officer stood guard with his rifle. Neither of the two could accept there was such a place as Wales; they peered and pondered and shook their heads. Anthony cleverly cut them short. He asked them if there was an albergo where we could stay the night. The man at the table suddenly chuckled in affable welcome, and told the officer to take us to the albergo.

My feet were printed on Italy; they were to return. The albergo was ramshackle, with only one room for travellers. It was stone-floored and cold as the grave. The enormous bed was a majestic catafalque of resplendent whiteness, white as the single candle beside it. Five stiff pillows were ranged along its head. Anthony wondered if we'd be expected to share the bed with other stray travellers. Such a prospect did not bother me; I was shivering with the gruesome cold of cold bones. Swilling my face in a washstand bowl was a wash in chips of marble. But there was promise of hot soup and an omelette downstairs. In the passage a thickset young servant girl fled precipitately from our approach. She had the facial cast and black curls of Turin-born Vanna, who had married me in the coke ovens at home.

It was difficult to believe that a score of miles southwards lay the pampered coast, with all its accomplished machinery for warm pleasures. In this creek of the racial mountains watchfulness remained sharp as an axe. The two grey-cloaked officers came in for a drink while we sat over our poor soup, flat omelette, dried figs and sour wine. They eyed us from inkspot eyes like ganders'. The rattling door opened and a wispy man with a pinched face of startling pallor entered, stood hesitatingly until we finished our omelette, then approached in deferential shyness. With palsied hands and in a leafy voice he offered for our inspection a few sheets of ruled paper, on each of which an Italian poem was written in an ornamental script and flourishingly signed. He was selling them. The poem I bought had to do, I found, with a bird in a tree.

'*Il poeta*,' explained one of the watching officers, after the spectre had gone; and he made a gesture towards his loins, and then to his Adam's apple. They accepted a drink from us and took their operatic plumage, cloaks and guns off into the night. They had decided we were not spies or bandits. Since both our passports declared us writers, had the local poet been instructed to visit us, either from courtesy or from observation of our reactions to verse?

Upstairs, the monumental bed crackled like breaking icicles as I sank into it. All the villagers, including the wolf officers, would have been welcome in it. Next day, after a long, long tramp, we limped into a small town, and there were better comforts, especially to eat. Mental torpor results from such climbs into wholesome heights. Scenic glories failed to register any more. On the third day we took a slow, fussy tram down to the Italian Riviera. Carnation-drenched Ventimiglia was healthy enough for me, my cheap room in Nice palatial, a mouse I sometimes saw in the kitchen a devoted old friend, and the arrogant monocle of Ernst an amusing little sun.

I completed my novel as my six months on the playful coast drew to a regretted close. A week of bad weather came in February. P.R. Stephensen, an Australian I knew who published *éditions-de-luxe* of classics and a literary magazine in London with Jack Lindsay, arrived in Nice and we went together to Bandol. Stephensen made arrangements to publish a high-priced book of Lawrence's paintings and also one of his best essays, *À Propos of Lady Chatterley's Lover* — a courageous venture, since other London publishers remained dubious of the incalculable author of the *Lady* and the Home Secretary's birch.

I counted my money — a little had turned up from ever-blessed America — and thought I had enough for a month in Paris. By March the Nice 'season' was finishing. Sybaritic Ernst retreated to his family estates. I packed my trunk. I gave Madame S a bottle of scent at the door of her apartment below, and was still not invited within; Ernst had told me not to present French people with handkerchiefs because of a superstition that it meant weeping to come, but in view of his opinion of the nation I should have thought that such a *faux pas* would be encouraged by him. For Mrs Cronin, Sister Beryl and even philosophic little Rosamund I was one of the many pieces of flotsam in their world-wide rovings, and our parting had no melancholy.

Lawrence had decided to visit Paris with me while Frieda went to Germany to see her relations. Not wanting to sustain the long journey at one go, he had booked a room for us in some quiet half-way town unknown to me. The train was a slow one. I felt he would have liked to travel in a wheelbarrow if someone would push it. Our trunks went on direct to Paris in the *rapide* Frieda took from Marseilles. On Marseilles station, where the three of us met, I had barely recognized Lawrence. Obtained in Toulon for this visit to the capital, he wore a curly-brimmed grey felt hat and a long, thick overcoat; at first glance he looked like a dimly goatish upholder of bourgeois principles.

The umbrella he carried was needed. Pouring rain and a raw wind of the wintry North whipped us in the dour town at which, long after dark, we alighted from our ambling train. The gloom of a shuttered French provincial town lowered my spirits further. The nightingale South lay in another country. A dank barouche and drenched horse took us to a half-hearted hotel. Other qualms came after dinner there. The large room Lawrence had booked contained a curtained-off space for bathroom. He took a bath before bed, did not close the front curtain, and, looking up from a book I was reading in bed, I caught a glimpse of him drying himself. A strange pang shot through me. It left an elusive sense of foreboding. I had never seen such a frail, wasted body, so vulnerable-looking. All the querulousness, finger-shaking lecturing, rampageous personal attacks and impatience of contemporary writers (and of Chekhov) were of no account.

This visual impact was deceptive. There was no wasting of the demoniac flame within that trapped white body. Nevertheless he should not have gone to Paris; he hated cities, and it was some-times a raw March during our month there. Frieda, passing through on the night before, had arranged for our two communicating rooms in the warm Hôtel de Versailles on the Boulevard Mont-parnasse, run by some Lawrence acquaintances, the sensible Madame Chaumier, her husband and their kindly American friend, Louis. Lawrence's search for a publisher for a cheap edition of *Lady Chatterley* began at once. (He predicted to me that

146

the unexpurgated book would be sold openly in England within ten years: thirty-five were to be needed.) Sylvia Beach, publisher of *Ulysses*, was the first person he approached in Paris.

In the taxi that took us to Miss Beach's bookshop in an obscure street one of Lawrence's excessive rages gripped him, alarming me despite its evidence of undiminished vitality. The taxi-driver, a big bull-necked man, couldn't find the street. As we cruised for the second time around the islanded Odéon Theatre Lawrence began to start and writhe. The powerful, unmoving back of the driver roused him to yelling, in English. 'The fat fool! A taxi-driver! Fool, fool, fool! Or else he's doing it on purpose, knowing we're foreigners.' A demented monkey squirmed and jerked on the seat beside me. The driver remained unperturbed. We went around the Odéon again. Lawrence's face was lifted in agony, ruddy beard stuck out. A crisis seemed to be at hand.

At last the shop was discovered and the taxi purred up to the kerb. Lawrence's thin body exploded out of the door. I followed in readiness for a pavement brawl. It did not come. The two men faced each other. The driver's large moony face shone with a childlike beam; it was all a friendly joke to him. In heavy French he told us he was a Russian, an exile, and had only recently begun his job as a taxi-driver. Lawrence had started back from that broad Slav face. His prancings were stilled. As we crossed to Miss Beach's shop, he said, 'I *couldn't* be angry with him. Did you see his face? Beautiful and human. He lives in his blood, that man, he's solidly in his blood. I saw it at once and I respected him.' I went for a walk while Miss Beach turned *Lady Chatterley*, and a small fortune, down. Publication of *Ulysses* had fulfilled her.

On sunny days we took short walks in Montparnasse, but Lawrence would not go to the cafés. ('No person of taste sits on café terraces,' he censured me one morning, forefinger brandished, after I had stayed out all night when Frieda had returned from Germany.) In the streets I noticed how passers-by would suddenly gaze, almost with a start, at his haggard, burning-eyed face under the formal hat. An international literary society, learning of his presence in Paris, wanted to arrange a dinner; he would not have it. When a friend made arrangements for him to see a specialist in lung diseases, he came into my room half an hour before the appointment, ready dressed for it, and asked me to telephone cancelling it. Did he believe that a submission to medical art was an act of treachery to the power within him, his gods?

At night I would wake to his coughings and restless movements in the next room. Once, instinctively, I hurried through the communicating door, and found him as though in mortal combat with some invisible opponent, the dark tormented face and thin body like some stormy El Greco figure writhing on the bed. He seemed to be violently repudiating an evil force, a wretched man nearly overcome by a sinister power of super-human advantages. I was frightened of a haemorrhage. His leather bag of homely medicines lay open beside his bed. When I suggested calling a doctor he flew into a rage. He asked me to sit quietly by the bed for a while. He needed the aid of some human presence. The fit of anger seemed to be good for him, and soon he was calmer, lay back exhausted, unspeaking but triumphant. The opponent had gone.

It was at such moments that I realized Frieda's value to him, the virtues of her lack of neurosis. I would not listen to the trenchant objections to her which a long-standing woman friend of his retailed to me in Paris. When Frieda returned from Germany I was out on some errand at the time of her afternoon arrival in the hotel. Returned, I knocked on Lawrence's door and was told to enter. The couple lay in bed under a tumbled counterpane of crimson velvet, Lawrence's bearded head nestling contentedly on a hearty bosom refreshed by a fortnight's breathing of its native air. One of the *Belle Epoque* painters could have depicted this *après midi* of mature connubial repose in an old-fashioned Paris bed. Frieda laughed at my bashfulness; I must have betrayed surprise at this haste. I had brought her a bar of Montélimar nougat, one of the many sweetmeats she adored, and we ate it there and then. I was glad she was back.

Unknown to Lawrence, I had kept her supplied with reports from Paris while she was in Germany. After my doubts of my capability to cope with such a man it was reassuring to read in a reply from Baden-Baden '... I was thankful for your letter. Lawrence says you are so nice with him. I can't remember that he ever said it of anybody else! I am not to worry about him, but I do — it's no use — I am grateful to have you there ....' But I felt the strain. Sometimes I stole out of the hotel late at night and hared up the short distance to the Dôme. The wild expatriate

Americans there were endlessly fascinating to me. They were battling, however squalidly, to shake hayseed out of their hair; in my case, it was coaldust.

In the daytime, Paris worked its handsome spell on me. I did not work, except for a poem of fifteen lines, the last ever to darken the threshold of my mind:

Louvre

I would give all my old razor-blades
and a heap of sous to have her altered,
the little vacuous lips particularly,
as she stands alone, almanacked and advertized
everywhere and in a few stale words
prettily bunched by the not-to-be-accounted-for
Walter Pater.

Behind her stand the eternal rocks, dark and beautiful,
as shadows for her fish-like smile,
the never-to-be-baked dough of her brow and cheeks
is Pater for the ends of the world
upon her head: and was he so subtle, Walter,
to delude so passionately?

The ascenseur is twenty centimes
to the upper floor of the Louvre.

The *Mona Lisa* was a great disappointment. Lawrence shook his head over my poem. But he was unexpectedly helpful with a short story of mine when he had met Edward Titus for discussion of an edition of *Lady Chatterley*. Titus, prosperous husband of Helena Rubinstein, edited a magazine in Paris, *This Quarter*; Lawrence took him my short story, and, calling later at the editor's office in a street behind the Dôme, I received a generous cheque. In pursuance of my policy of ridding Anglo-Welsh writing of flannel and bringing some needed flesh tints to it, my story had to do with a naked bourgeois wife opening the front door of her house and finding there, instead of her expected husband, a startled young miner whose own Baptist chapel wife had never granted him such a dazzling treat. Called *Revelation*, I had written the story one evening after listening to Madame S's rites of Venus in the room next to mine in Nice.

149

Negotiations for the Titus edition of *Lady Chatterley* were settled before Frieda returned, and Lawrence was his amusing best at a lunch party for six he gave in a modest Montparnasse restaurant. His illness seemed non-existent on that sunny spring day; he took expert charge of the carving of two roast fowls, establishing with the admiring waiter his instant understanding of all persons. Aldous Huxley arrived at a house in Suresnes and took him off there for two or three days' rest from Montparnasse. Invited there to lunch, I found Lawrence talking almost without stop at the table, a guest famous — and unresented — for his bountiful outgiving. Tall, graceful-mannered Huxley, his Belgian wife and a deftly-soothing Englishwoman were contrastingly subdued. Acquainted with Lawrence in the past, these old friends of his were concerned, I discovered, at the marked change in his physical appearance.

So I was relieved when Frieda returned and I saw the disputatious pair cosily established in bed at mid-afternoon. I stayed a while longer at the hotel, vacating my room for Frieda and moving to another across the corridor. Sometimes we had money-saving picnics in her room. She would go out with a basket and return with delicious paté and vegetable salads which we ate from paper napkins and cartons; cheese, apples, one of those long batons of bread, and wine in our tooth glasses, made the feasts all the more festal for Frieda's broad *hausfrau* gaiety and her eye for the best items in food shops. She had brought a nephew with her from Germany, one of the Richthofens, and he too shed the comely glow she possessed.

I longed for England and Wales now. One can suddenly get one's fill of a foreign country, its alien chatter and food, its bad habits and shortcomings, and I did not care for Parisians as much as for the southerners. I packed my trunk. In its depth, under a top tray, lay a final draft of those troublesome *Pansies*, including recent additions dotted with a few vulgar words. I was to deliver them in London; Lawrence still suspected the British authorities of interfering with his mail (accurately, as it turned out). Also hidden under my clothes was an expensive early copy of Norman Douglas's *Limericks*, published in Florence; Douglas had sent it to me in Nice at the request of a London friend of mine and had warned me of possible Customs seizure. Lawrence, his former friend, had dipped into this coarse book with a finicky wrinkling of his nose.

We had a final restaurant meal. It did not occur to me for an instant that I would not see Lawrence again. He talked of going to England in the summer. People came and went casually in the life of this endlessly travelling pair. The husband had brought a sense of halt into my own life. And my six months in France had been rewarding. But I was glad to be going back to Britain. I could never settle 'abroad' myself.

When I reached Victoria station, travelling by the cheap Dieppe/ Newhaven route, I collected my trunk for Customs inspection of registered luggage and stood at a counter in the shed with the normal air of detachment common to culprits. The officer asked me to open up. He glanced at the top tray of garments, packed by a person clearly of orderly habits. How long had I been abroad? Your passport, please? He slowly turned the pages, looked at me sharply, returned the passport, and removed the top tray of my trunk. The crook on the wrong side of the counter mourned for the sheaf of fresh-faced *Pansies*. Like the Home Secretary snatching an earlier spray from the Postmaster-General's trembling hand, would this officer know all about the poisonous little horrors? Surely not? Probably it was the *Limericks* that would get me into trouble here. An engine-whistle shrieked a sudden blast nearby. Childhood guilt prickled my flesh. The officer shifted a few garments about, turned my espadrilles over. Was a Black Maria waiting in the station yard? But the blind paws below my vacant eye did not delve deeper into the trunk. A stub of chalk scribbled its compliment on the rear end.

Our Customs sheds are palaces of magic adventure for me to this day. I would not have their guardians thrown into a harbour. The charm of a trip abroad would lose a Gilbert and Sullivan antic if those interrogators were abolished. It is a joy to witness a foreign woman, especially if she is French, do her stuff for the cement-faced male hags. A Customs shed at boat-time would make a good subject for a ballet. Even when, arriving at Dover from Switzerland on one occasion, I was taken to a dirty cabin and had all my person carefully searched (I had already paid £3 duty on a Swiss watch I had honestly declared at the counter), the performance seemed to me entertaining and the officer's apology a pleasing bit of British humbug. And, after all, I *had* smuggled in those *Pansies* years before; so in a way the public hauling off to a filthy cabin was tit-for-tat.

Six: One or Two Bloomsbury Ornaments

L
ondon seemed full of other robust little ways. I was back in the pub, British Museum and poached eggs routine of my happy apprenticeship. The subtle change of London atmosphere that followed the General Strike of 1926 was rather more noticeable, though the juggernaut of unemployment was not yet in full procession. Money was shorter; and I had almost none left. Publishers were less adventurous. They quibbled, rightly, over my second novel, and I set to the dustman toil of clearing away the rubbish in it.

Until some money turned up I stayed at the Fitzroy Square flat of my painter friend, yellow-haired Eve Kirk, occupying her brother's room while he was away. She would come in from a day's painting of her Thames-side subjects and, much impressing me, immediately lie flat on her hard studio floor, recovering in this disciplined and draughty position, she alleged, complete stamina and resilience. Such a relaxation did not seem beneficial for a writer; my mind kept galloping long after I left the workbench which writers seldom leave even in sleep. Painters struck me as needing minds for their toil much less than writers. Vision and craft seemed to suffice them. They could put their canvases out of sight and forget professional problems in their exuberant recreational indulgences. I was always jealous of painters.

I seldom met with such unruffled poise in a woman as Eve Kirk possessed. It can be seen in Augustus John's harmonious portrait of her, *The Pink Girl*. John, more than twice her age, came to the Fitzroy Square flat one evening. Darkly craggy, he looked a battered Welsh castle of a man, built to withstand all assaults from time, women and bottles none the less. He was already a mythical figure to my generation. Despite the Don Juan and wild gipsy element in the myth, there seemed to be, as far as I could detect, no true sensuality in him, save in a functional way that had not been rusted by cynicism or rancidity. Now and again the croak of a benevolent raven came from him. After he had gone, bemused Eve said to me, 'You have met the greatest man of our time.' I much liked his drawings.

Unwittingly I brought Eve's flat into disrepute during my stay. Both of us were out (in the circumstances, was this known?) when one afternoon, on a pretext that the flat was reported to be a distribution place for copies of *Lady Chatterley's Lover*, a couple of police detectives gained access to our open top-floor through Curtis Moffat's interior decorating premises below. I had been in correspondence with Lawrence from the address; the *Pansies* had been taken to their destination, and printing of a 'private' edition was under way. Others of Lawrence's London correspondents were similarly molested at the time. There was no *Lady Chatterley* in Eve Kirk's flat, or anything else that could start a blush on a policeman's cheek; there was merely evidence of honest toil with paintbrush and pen and two pigeons we had left cooking in a slow oven.

Parochial parties were becoming less obstreperous in Bloomsbury, though the heyday of that quarter was not yet finished. The wilder figures continued to pack such pubs as the Fitzroy, with everlasting Nina Hamnett a daily news-sheet of everybody's fortune and fate. One of Bloomsbury's virtues lay in its strong democratic structure; this counterbalanced the atmosphere of hothouse exclusiveness generated by the original settlers such as Virginia Woolf and Lytton Strachey. Much of the area pleasing to the eye, especially the Squares, it had too the usefulness of a compact geographical boundary; there was always a hospitable roof under which could be found someone with whom to at least discourse. Ruination could be earned, as elsewhere, and the renowned drunks of Bloomsbury were as dreary as those in the Rhondda. A night in the Fitzroy required stamina. When the bleak old man of the poverty-stricken Thirties arrived in London with his scythe he did not neglect visits to that sticky hive, and an evening there then could be more expensive than one at the Ritz.

A half-hypnotized scourge of the parish, and all it stood for, was the talked-of South African poet, Roy Campbell. Ever in and out of Bloomsbury from his home in the Camargue, he was reputed to be an amateur bullfighter in the Provençal festivals — 'Oh, yes,' said Eve, who shared his love of the Camargue and Provence, 'Roy *did* leap into a village square once, waving an hotel towel at some frightened old beast.' He too, like Hemingway, fostered hair on the chest. His scorn of aesthetes' cabals and the preciosity of inner Bloomsbury seemed understandable. Less attractive was the braggadocio in his temperament. He came to the Fitzroy Square flat to dinner, and the talk was of contemporary poets. Campbell took pleasure in relating how, a few months before, he had kicked a young man guest from the Camargue house ('I *kicked* him out of the door and down the steps') after discovering that this hard-drinking American, Hart Crane, had been attempting to corrupt the uncorrupted local fishermen. The name of the American poet was unknown to me at the time. A year or two later Crane threw himself out of a ship into the Caribbean and, it was reported, waved a hand before disappearing to Neptune's arms. Campbell, ever resolute in opposing the ideals of Bloomsbury intellectuals, was to become a fervid supporter of Franco in the approaching terrors of the Spanish civil war.

Occasionally, Eve and her brother Geoffrey took me to their parents' home in Hampshire. Such traditional English retreats for week-ends were new to my Rhondda breeding. Theirs was a rambling house in a hoary village, with the last of the race of white-capped domestics ghostly in passages, and a walled rose-garden, strawberries ripening under nets, walks in tranquil woods or beside a trout stream. True old England breathed in such orderly pauses in time. Eve and Geoffrey's mother made her own hats, sewing on to them glossy green leaves plucked from a laurel bush, or bronze-red ones from an October beech. Her long flowing dresses, romantically bygone, in no way interfered with her mastery of a decrepit motor-car's temperamental innards; lying in the dust of a road at repairs, she was a Ronald Firbank figure. Burne-Jones drawings of her as a girl hung on her walls. She told me about a stubborn old woman in the ancient local almshouses who resented installation of modern W.C.'s there and, forming a Lysistrata-like union of the other inmates against the Rural Council bigwigs, 'refused to sit over water'. It provided me with a reasonably popular short story.

I couldn't really afford the Bloomsbury life. Most of the people I associated with there were established in earning capacity or had private means derived from the middle-class security which still was the backbone of this England. Bloomsbury was helpful, with its women, of course, far more understanding than men in the delicate matter of finding the wherewithal to live. I was friendly with a well-off woman novelist — well-off from her important husband, not her stark novels, in which everybody ended in sordid disaster — whose splendid dinners *en famille* brought a little fat to my cheeks. Save for the awful puritanism which I could not completely rid myself of, there was no drastic need for me to abscond from Bloomsbury. But once more I began the peregrinations to cheap bed-sitting rooms elsewhere. Guilt has many hovels for our redemptive occupation.

My novel still hung fire; second novels are bastards. I became ashamed of being poor. I would not borrow money even from my parents, and when D.H. Lawrence heard of my plight from a friend and sent a cheque for ten pounds I stupidly refused it. Yet I did not get into debt. When the lurid red light appeared I went nimbly to ground, saw nobody, and could spend a month equably without speaking to a soul. Now and again a tiny sum arrived for a story in the little magazines that still wasted their sweetness on the larger desert air; also, there was a period craze of 'private press' limited editions of a story — tarted-up productions, each copy numbered and signed by the author and 'collected' by abnormal customers who usually were blissfully unconcerned with the text. To be paid twenty pounds or so for a hundred signatures seemed dotty, though welcome, to me. I plodded along. The thudding footsteps of the near Thirties were still faint.

Meanwhile, in the summer of 1929, Frieda Lawrence had come to London for the exhibition of her husband's paintings at the Warren Gallery in Maddox Street. The irrepressible official persecutors took another dab at the irrepressible sex crusader, and so the ding-dong went on and on. Seizure of a dozen pictures resulted in many thousands of men and women visiting the attenuated exhibition. After the police raid Dorothy Warren gave an evening party at her gallery. The blank spaces on the walls somehow conveyed rebuke, if not depression. Frieda, resplendent in an evening gown, a spray of pure white lilies on a Junoesque shoulder, was of course guest of honour. Main joke of the evening was the raiders' wish to seize a William Blake print, the original of which was an exhibit at the Tate Gallery. Dorothy Warren waited until dignified Frieda had left before she leapt on to a table and gave a roaring speech of left-wing defiance, accompanied by a clenched-fist maenad dance.

Her aunt, Lady Ottoline Morrell, was not there, but Frieda took me to meet the celebrated Bloomsbury hostess at her Gower Street house. I knew little of the breach in the Lawrence's friendship with her, except that Lady Ottoline had taken offence at the portrayal of her as Hermione Roddice in *Women in Love* and that neither D.H. nor Frieda had seen her since publication of the novel. Frieda and I were taken by a maid to an upstairs boudoir. Lady Ottoline, magnificently past her prime, stood tall and erect in a theatrically rich costume which, with its stiffly upright back-collar and many ropes of pearls, reminded me of some portrait of Queen Elizabeth. Hair of reddish hues lay strewn about her equine, remarkably boned face. Her eyes pondered on one slowly, her personal questions had a penetrating inquisitiveness; if a marvellous racehorse could have spoken it would have been with this high-bred basic curiosity.

An air of reserve was maintained between the two women; they appeared to be carefully skirting around each other's politeness. Frieda sat with a *grande dame* pensiveness she could summon up when put to it. It was interesting to me to meet the 'original' of Hermione Roddice. She had seemed to me by far the most visually living character in my favourite *Women in Love*; and, now, Hermione seemed to me a most successful example of the difficult art of using living models for a novelist's purpose. In ambience and to the eye at least, Lawrence's copy had wonderful acumen. I could not assess the truth of Hermione's writhing inner torments in the novel; that Ottoline/Hermione drama, if any, lay in the past. This afternoon there was a calm atmosphere of all passion gone from the offended original. Lawrence was to pay tribute to his subject in one of his letters — 'She is like an old, tragic queen who knows that her life has been spent in conflict with a kingdom that was not worth her life.' He thought her one of the 'great spirits' of Europe.

She preceded us down the staircase after our private audience in the boudoir, and I have never seen a staircase put to its use so regally. In a ground-floor room, awaiting her entrance, were half a dozen habitués of her weekly 'afternoon'. A copper kettle steamed on an oval table, and there were buns and jam. Lady Ottoline made tea; we sat formally around the table. James

Stephens, the fey Irish poet and *Crock of Gold* novelist, did not stop bubbling airy-fairy words; diminutive, a creature liable to pop out from under ferns to annoy people with moonshine loquacity, a literary Ireland bedevilled the table. I was placed next to him, perhaps because I was Welsh, but was able to reflect that the Welsh are, thank heaven, clear of Celtic feyness. Frieda remained detached and, by contrast, judiciously down-to-earth.

From Majorca, which she and Lawrence visited after the scandal of the Warren Gallery raid had faded, her husband wrote me, '... A man pinched Frieda's bottom on the tram — I wasn't there — don't tell her I told you — so she despises every letter in the word Majorca and is rampant to sail to Italy, where her squeamish rear has never been pinched.' He seemed gayer in his letters just then. The dread of losing his seized pictures gone, he wrote yet more retaliatory *Pansies*, had an idea of launching a satirical little periodical, to be called *The Squib*, and suggested I should be editor. He thought I would be good at squibs. The idea was set aside.

It seemed impossible that this ceaselessly productive man was approaching his end. But I did not like an undernote in one of his later letters to me, when he and Frieda had returned to Bandol, renting a furnished house there — 'I have been wanting all this time to write, but my bronchials have been giving me such a bad time. Now I'm in bed with linseed poultices, so can't go much lower. There was a great storm yesterday — huge seas — today is quiet, but grey and chill and forlorn; imagine me the same ....' Linseed poultices! I remembered his little leather bag of simple remedies and the avoidance of a doctor in Paris.

That he consented to be taken from Bandol to the Ad Astra sanatorium at Vence must have been an ominous abandonment of belief in his private gods. He was forty-four. Leaving the British Museum one afternoon, I saw on the poster of an evening paper, *Death of D.H. Lawrence,* and for some minutes couldn't bring myself to overcome an instant denial of this death and read the paper. It would have been better not to have read it, or most of the obituaries in other papers in the next days, with their raw proof of this death. Only the *Manchester Guardian* and the *Times Literary Supplement* were truthful and warm in their tributes to Lawrence as a writer and a person. The others were indecent. The phoenix was beaten to *their* kind of death in his nest.

It was early March. Some days before he died I had written to Frieda asking for news, saying he must greet the spring triumphantly as before and reminding her of the day when we had taken the Bandol droshky into the countryside and found the first anemones. She replied, 'No, you won't make him a chaplet of anemones any more, but anemones crown his grave now. His death was so simple and somehow great, his courage in facing death and fighting inch by inch and then at the end asking for morphia. He looked so proud, so beyond all these silly ugly dogs barking, so unconquered when he was dead — I know you grieve too.'

Seven: Caerphilly Jones,
A Sprig of the Thirties

After further rewriting, my second novel had been accepted by my turnabout publishers — the firm had changed hands, its original founders, the three idealistic young men down from Cambridge, having taken to their heels before the times had darkened into the Thirties. I had a fortune to draw on. One could swagger on £75 advance payment then. But I began to learn a lesson about money. This was easier because of my ability to stay retreated into my various holes without too much grizzling or depression, sallying out for prowls — mostly nocturnal — only occasionally.

The advance payment in hand, I took a long, cool 'studio' room on the ground floor of a massive old house standing isolated in a garden lying off the bottom of Haverstock Hill. Karl Marx had spent his last years in a terraced house up the quiet road beyond my laurel hedge. The studio had its own side-entrance in the laurels; there was a trellised patio, a huge stone bathroom, a small kitchen, and a coal-grate in the long room. It cost £1 per week, and a Cockney charwoman 2s. 6d. for two hours, talk included. I soon got rid of its mice; perhaps the last of some Stone Age breed, they had extraordinarily long tails. Gillyflowers and asters filled the patio coffers. My favourite bed-reading became fat cookery books, soothing fantasy at such an hour, an apparitional range of elaborate dishes lapsing into dreams not to be fulfilled.

An extra sum of money came from America for a short story, and I went on a trip to Germany with the native Charles Lahr, H.E. Bates, and the painter William Roberts, who seldom stopped reading a pocket New Testament. The Nazi movement was to be detected but seemed merely a turbulence of swollen-headed youths. Otherwise the country had a relaxed atmosphere still exhausted by war-defeat, and it was certainly poor economically. The boisterous German humour could be a trial. In a Rhineland village the woman innkeeper, an Amazonian widow, slipped a

159

lump of ice into my open-necked shirt at the back as I sat in the garden. She wanted me to stay on free of charge in return for teaching her English and help make her calendar-picture inn an attraction for British tourists. Everywhere we went we found great respect for England.

A resident of Mainz took me, at my request, to a well-conducted brothel. Ripe ladies in various states of dowdy undress sat in a downstairs salon, most of them talking with family-looking men over glasses of beer. There was a frowsty atmosphere of solemn confabulations. The routine for a newcomer consisted of selecting an inmate, then a brief consultation with the ample *hausfrau*, who conducted one formally up a staircase outside the salon, the selected woman following after one had been left alone in a bedroom for, presumably, a few minutes of meditation or preparation. Presently I sat in a cosy, very home-like room with a woman attired in a corset and frilly-edged drawers which could be called bloomers.

I had chosen her downstairs at random. She was about forty. My Mainz acquaintance had understood my vulgar professional curiosity in wanting to visit a German brothel, and, uninterested himself, he remained waiting below with a beer and a newspaper. I knew almost no German. Everything went wrong. The substantial corset and the frilly drawers, although fresh-laundered, upset me. Soon after their wearer had come into the room she asked for her pay. It was a very reasonable sum. I remained on a straight-backed chair at a table covered with a plush cloth. The bed looked spick-and-span. After tucking her money inside her corset-top, the woman opened an album of photographs on the table. There were staid family groups; she pointed to a photograph of a baby, then to between her thighs, and I understood the child was hers and she was obliged to support it. I lost all interest and remained at the table. Nonplussed, she fetched a short black whip from the back of an enormous picture hanging on the wall and made an inquiring gesture towards her behind. I shook my head. Did the corset reach down so far? Perhaps I ought to have found out. I tried to convey as gallantly as I could that I wanted nothing. She was not a whit put out. We descended with the same etiquette-observance as my ascent with the *hausfrau*. I wondered if this was the only brothel in town. My Mainz cicerone did not appear to possess the German sense of humour. Or did he?

Before proceeding to Berlin we stayed three or four days at a farmhouse remote from Mainz, the home of Lahr, and were mowed down by the friendliness and glut of food. A welcoming party was given us at the village inn. A huge, constantly replenished glass boot foaming with beer was passed in strict rotation from mouth to mouth of all the men, while the buxom women stood apart and beamed. H.E. Bates, offering to escort a girl home, found her watchful aunt dogging their long walk at a discreet distance. The countryside rolled with powerful grain and huge pigs. The richest farmer invited us to use the bathroom he had proudly installed, the only one in the area; we went there, took our turns, and found a banquet prepared for us, with yet more hot pork chops, two or three for each of us. There seemed to be no wrecked Germany here.

With two other companions, I was to go again to incalculable Germany a couple of years later, stopping in Cologne *en route* to Berlin. Cologne appeared to be brisk and thriving on that trip. Everything in our large hotel near the railway station hummed with confident efficiency. The meals in its packed restaurant were colossal and served with tremendous zeal. One lunchtime I watched a boy of about nine go around the tables with a collecting box. Dressed in a smart replica of a military uniform, complete with glistening jackboots, he clicked his heels and bowed stiffly before each table. Nobody ignored the box. The erect little automaton, much admired by the diners, was collecting for the Hitler *Jugend*.

The next day I was held up in a wide shopping street by a gigantic procession of Brownshirts. At its approach a peculiar silence descended on the crowded thoroughfare, which had been closed to vehicles. Only the sharp tramp of boots could be heard in the docile quiet. Phalanx after phalanx marched with magnificent precision, endless columns of curt-faced men, all alike in expression. I was alone and due at a café on the other side of the street; I waited, then decided to dash across the road through a division in the interminable formations. Fleet of foot though I am, I had not reached the opening before an angry babble of shouts came from the spectators lining the kerb. I had insulted the display of might. Nevertheless I skipped on, though half mesmerized by a row of lifted boots advancing towards me. I got through safely. Staring faces at the opposite kerb were hostile, but I was received in silence. It was realized I was an ignorant tourist.

An instance of the diligent honesty of this strange race came after we boarded a train at Cologne for Berlin. I had told my chambermaid at the hotel that I was going there. The train was about to move when, standing in the corridor, I saw a page-boy from the hotel running along the platform, scanning the windows and holding aloft a pair of shoes. They were an uncomfortable pair I had decided to discard and had left beside the wastepaper basket in my room. The boy saw me as the train moved; I waved my hand rejectingly. I could not imagine such consideration from a French hotel.

In Berlin there was no evidence of the Cologne militarism. But it was an oppressive capital; one's wings wouldn't open there, as in Paris. The national talent for circumspect dowdiness lay thick in the atmosphere. But in a small bookshop which I had been told to visit, the proprietor, after I mentioned the name of a London friend, produced an elaborate book of George Grosz cartoons, banned by the Nazis. It was *Ecce Homo*, grim, rasping, ruthless depictions of coarsely depraved German types. I bought it at a moderate price — the Jewish proprietor seemed glad to be shot of it from his premises.

It was hard to know what to do with oneself in Berlin. The Eldorado night-club still functioned, like the antics in the thoroughfares around it. I had not visited it on my previous German trip. I danced with a slight, pretty girl who spoke excellent English. She had sat with her encouraging middle-aged American escort at a table next to one where I and my two English male companions endeavoured to seem at home. 'You know she's a man?' one of my friends said when I returned to our table. I had half suspected it on the floor. Most of the other dancing 'women' did not need a second look. We invited our neighbours to a drink at our table. The girl, very pleased by my doubt, readily admitted to his sex and told me that he and his escort had been travelling by car all over Europe as a married pair — 'except', he said, a gruff note coming teasingly into his light voice, 'when we're arriving at a frontier. Then I go into the back of the car and change into men's clothes — it's less fussy than explaining to officials that my passport is really me. If we get our luggage examined they stare a bit at all my frocks and my three wigs, but they're used to everything.'

I did not ask which sex he adopted when registering at hotels.

162

He said he had been born in Cornwall and had emigrated to America with his parents at fourteen. He looked discreet enough in his simple black frock, necklet of pearls, bobbed auburn wig and accomplished make-up. I felt that he was boss in the association; his authoritative composure indicated it. The escort, a manic-depressive type, had the fixity of an experienced alcoholic who never gets drunk in a celebrating manner but continues like an unstopping railway engine sweeping through endless flat prairies. After our glasses of ordinary hock he insisted on ordering two bottles of champagne. He swallowed pills. I imagined solid family money in America, a doting mother, not a day's work done by her son, and a complete breakdown of faculties, if not suicide, when desire failed him and the day terrified and the doors of his face would not open. My native evangelism had not gone. That American probably ended up on the board of a corporation.

We left the Eldorado couple long after midnight. Out in the streets I was not so fooled by the many perambulating hussies in their tatty masquerades, a few of them outrageously impudent, others funny as *Charley's Aunt*. I felt again that German humour, if it is to be appreciated by a foreigner, requires a philosophic distance from it. Perhaps it is clinically necessary for the nation, a detergent for German sentimentality and its obverse of cruelty. The Germans pass a steamroller over sex matters. One returns from visits to their country without exhilaration, but certainly thoughtful. Returned from this second trip, I wrote a censorious short story, *Cherry Blossom on The Rhine*, which, after publication in the *London Mercury*, appeared in translation in France and the Scandinavian countries and, although not a well-composed piece, in Edward O'Brien's annual *Best Short Stories*, published in England and America. It ridiculed the Hitler *Jugend* and the new Germany. I sent a copy to Ernst, my friend of Nice days, whom I had not met since. He had settled down at his Hamburg home.

A letter of severe rebuke arrived from him. My story was ridiculous, the shallow view of a foreigner in a tourists' Rhine Valley. What could I know of the real Hitler *Jugend* in a week or two of holiday? My young German on the Rhine boat was idiotic except for his remarks on Jews and racial purity in marriage. Instead of going on to decadent and international Berlin in my holiday why hadn't I come to his district? I must come. He would show me the true, the real people at work building a new Germany that would last. Unemployment and poverty were being conquered. I had been fooled. He was shocked.

Ernst enclosed a snapshot of himself in the letter. I could barely detect the elegant, monocled French Riviera habitué in this waxwork figure of combative stance and bristling moustache, a belt diagonally across its shirt, full stomach protruding from disreputable breeches, the handle of a knife visible above a jackboot. My hygienic Nice idler had become a Stormtrooper! It seemed much more ridiculous than my slipshod story. I remembered him shedding tears when sentimental Schubert pieces were played in the Jardins Albert bandstand; and also his blazing disgust at mean French indifference to sewerage deposited too close to the shore — 'I tread on it when I take my morning bathe!' he would shout on the Promenade des Anglais. I did not reply to his letter, and never heard from him again.

Caerphilly Jones saw the snapshot on my mantelshelf, and said, 'That chap looks as if he'd cut the throats of a dozen boy scouts before breakfast.'

Caerphilly did not know I had given him the name of the delicate cheese, a slice of which he was toasting on a long wire fork before the coal fire in my studio room below Hampstead's green heights. He couldn't have enough of the cheese, and, ever hungry, would eat half a pound at a sitting. I knew a Welsh dairy shop in Bloomsbury where the genuine native product could be obtained. Eating Caerphilly cheese, Jones was back home, more or less.

This white cheese, now degraded in factory manufacture, was especially delicious toasted in inch-thick slices at a coal fire and eaten with a little pepper and no mustard. There is a legend that the only Welshmen in Heaven were decoyed inside by the odour of toasting cheese, but whether it was Caerphilly or not is unknown. St Cecilia, badly needing some fresh male voices for an annual festival in honour of Creation, consulted St David about the Welsh. Why did those melodious Welsh circling in the outer darkness refuse to enter Heaven? St David thought they were frightened that they could not play rugby football in Heaven because it was always Sunday there. But he advised St Peter to toast some cheese at a fire just inside the Everlasting Gates. The wile succeeded. Such a crowd sprinted to the opened gates, bounding inside before St Peter slammed and locked-up, that Heaven never lacked champion choir-singing thereafter.

Caerphilly Jones, as I had nicknamed him to myself, hailed from one of the first of the mining valleys to become 'distressed' after the 1926 strike. He could sing, but was much more interested in food. Although it was to be some time before I met his family in Wales, I well knew his breed. In my father's shop I had seen people like his mother and father, and sometimes their lodger colliers, sampling the cheeses, staple food for pit tommy-tins. The cheap, strong Canadian cheeses were preferred to mild, dearer Caerphilly, which was a more feminine kind or for special occasions. Jones would eat Caerphilly in his weekly visit to me as if that day was his birthday.

I had first met him in a train when I was returning to London from one of my periodic visits to the deteriorating Rhondda Valley. He was twenty then, a trooper returning from leave. Iberian-dark, misleadingly glowering, he always remained lean and lithe despite his insatiable eating. Did his appetite stem from the bad times that, as he entered adolescence, began to gnaw at his small home valley? Did he want to catch up? He said he had joined the army to get some food. He had spent a year in the pit-stables of the local colliery before it went on half-time, with entire closure threatening. The Household Cavalry took him in of their charity. He loved horses, and ate like one.

He had other hungers. At some time in his adolescence he had heard the Wedding March from *Lohengrin* and the excerpt had stuck in his head, much as Beardsley's *Salome* drawings had in mine. Learning that the opera was to be performed at the Old Vic, he became obsessed with seeing it. He had never been in a theatre. I booked two seats and, spruce in the civvy suit he was allowed to wear by then, he came up from the Windsor barracks where he was stationed.

Lilian Baylis stood in her Old Vic foyer as usual, scrutinizing her arriving flock like a forbidding headmistress. In all my visits to the Old Vic I had not smelled the kipper she was reputed to be in the habit of frying on an oil-stove in the wings during her low-priced, under-staffed provision of Shakespeare and opera for the people. But after the opening performance of one of her seasons she had appeared before the curtain in scholastic gown and mortarboard — she had been given an honorary doctorate recently — and roundly censured us for not coming often enough. She told us exactly what the cash loss the previous season had been. Did we see the house on any but opening night? She very nearly called us a useless lot of hypocrites. I could believe the story that she had scolded Queen Mary in the foyer with, 'Why haven't you brought your husband?'

Caerphilly Jones was the sort of person she campaigned for. But *Lohengrin* overpowered him. Eyes glassy, he endured the long, long ordeal with soldierly rigidity. 'I didn't expect to see a swan,' he complained outside, cured of opera for ever. Soon he was cured of his boxing ambitions too. Glamorganshire, stable of so many boxers, did not produce a champion in him. After some training in his regiment he was selected to appear in a series of bouts between police and military at Shepherd's Bush Baths. He forbade me to go. A lack of confidence made him jumpy; he wanted to be anonymous, blindly sorting out deficiencies inside himself, a young man still lost in an alien land. I went to Shepherd's Bush Baths, hiding myself in the cheap seats of a crowded gallery. Caerphilly Jones's bout was stopped after its second round. Even to my untutored eye he was a donkey at boxing. In aspect rosily well-fed all his life, the policeman he fought had floored him.

'The boxing was a washout,' he said, toasting cheese the following week. I told him I was there. He hesitated, frowning, then smiled, pleased by this native support. 'I fancied myself as a glee-singer once,' he said, turning the cheese. 'But I had to go down-under straight from school. How was I to know the pit was going to chuck me and nearly everybody out? Then it was too late. No bloody glee-singing for anybody.' He sent home pathetically small postal orders from his miserable trooper's pay.

He told me of an obstinate old woman living alone in a house next door to his family. A great hand at growing ferns and other plants on her front parlour window-sill, she received one Christmas an important-looking bulb in a wadding-lined box. It had been sent by her granddaughter, who had gone adventuring to London and was assumed to be in service there. Impressed by the great size of this bulb, the granny planted the gift in a canister of soil from her back garden, frilling it with pink paper for her sill. But after a week or two visiting neighbours began to exclaim — 'What's this funny smell coming from your parlour? Is there something going bad?' 'It's Jinny's bulb from London,' the granny said. 'Watering him regularly I am. He'll come, he'll come in the spring.' It was Dr Watkins, summoned by neighbours to look at the declining old woman, who revealed the truth: 'Good God, it's a pineapple, woman! Same as the chunks in the tins.' But the granny was unmoved. 'Green leaves there are on the top,' she pleaded. 'He'll come, he'll come. A big flower there'll be in the spring, you'll see!' She did not live to see the miracle; and when smartly-dressed Jinny, her only relative, came down to bury her, of course the women of the terrace soon sniffed why she could afford to post such exotic presents from London.

Only part of Caerphilly Jones had come to London, and three years were to elapse before that part did well for itself and, gradually, absorbed the piece that had been left in Wales. Meanwhile, the foul Depression moved into full stride down there. Young people left the mining valleys in droves. Men of all ages tramped or hitch-hiked to London to forage for jobs; sometimes, mysterious as a pattern of dark-capped mushrooms, a circular group of them would appear in Oxford Street and, backs to the shoppers and heads down, a resonant harmony would rise from the dark ring, undepleted and not to be disregarded. Caerphilly Jones had taken a short cut by his enlistment — and into a hoarily crack regiment — but his solution left him vaguely restless and subject to bouts of sombre dejection. A wild resentment would scud through his dark, pre-Celtic eye. 'We get treated like big babies,' he complained of his barrack life. 'Don't do this, don't do that.' I assumed he hankered for the democracy of his native land.

Brooding over work in hand as I strolled in the Park alongside Knightsbridge one spring evening, I was startled to hear a voice bawling in my direction: *'Shw mae? Caws Caerffili gartref?'* The Welsh words, archaic-sounding in the circumstances, came from a misty cavalcade of slowly trotting black horses and troops, unrecognizable within plumed helmets and silver breastplates. They were returning from Whitehall duty. I might have been whisked back into medieval times. When I next saw Caerphilly Jones he said he had been sharply reprimanded for his flouting of the dignified ritual. He had merely greeted me and asked if I had Caerphilly cheese at home.

Later that year, I woke in the middle of the night in the divan at the end of my long studio room. Footsteps began to shuffle down the room. I could see a moving shadow. A burglar! I always left my window on to the patio open a few inches; its dim lower half was wide open now. An overhead light was suddenly switched on and I saw a pair of dust-smudged hands, then the dirty face of a man in khaki uniform. 'Come on, wake up! I'm starving. What's wrong with your bell?' The door bell had been out of order for a week. Caerphilly Jones had scaled the wall behind my laurel hedge.

He was on the run from something other than military discipline. Bunking from a country retreat where an annual training was proceeding for a month, he had thumbed lifts to London in lorries. He needed fodder without delay. I had no cheese. I placed a whole jam-filled Swiss roll on a plate with a knife, went into the kitchen to light the gas, and returned. The ten-inch Swiss roll had vanished in as many seconds, probably whole. He ate half a pound of bacon, eggs, tomatoes and fried bread, rummaged in the kitchen and found two stale rock buns. Marginally, he remarked that he did not intend returning to the army, and I realized why he had deposited his civilian suit at my premises just before going on his training stint in the country. But why had he waited until now to do a bunk?

He hedged. 'Oh, no, I haven't done anything bad,' he said. But if I lent him the train fare to Wales he could hide at his auntie's house in Ynyshir until they stopped bothering to search for the deserter; there were plenty of men to take his place nowadays. He couldn't stand the bull of army life any more. I told him the recent dire unemployment figures for Wales and the forebodings of further decline. 'Aye,' he said dismissingly and, fed, sang '*Y Deryn Pur*' in the bath.

In the clarity of mid-morning, I said, 'You had better go back. They'll find you.' Then he confessed that the day before he had received a letter from a girl telling him that she was almost certain she had 'clicked'. I felt relieved. But, although I accepted the classic pattern of his villainous urge to decamp from the trite old situation, there was the moral angle to consider. There was also the pursuing hand of authority, from the grasp of which he bamboozled himself the hidden valleys of Wales would be immune — I pressed this point, with the comparatively useless moral one a distance behind. I asked what kind of girl she was. I imagined a typical soldiers' moll. Or, if she was in love with this darkling thrush, was she attempting an old trick?

'I was the first,' he asserted primly. 'It was in Epping Forest on a Sunday this June — she lives not far off from there, Leytonstone way. Then she started coming west once a week to meet me. A girl she knows let us use her room down Victoria. Works in the Civil Service, her friend. Met them in a dance in barracks first.' Gloom settled on him, which made me feel I was virtuously achieving recognition of the moral angle. 'Maureen's clean and tidy,' he admitted. 'Works for her father. He's got a little business of his own, making mattresses for shops. Cockneys.'

At least he had had the tact not to ask to borrow my premises for their purpose. 'Well,' I said, 'it might be a false alarm. Sometimes it is. You'd better wait.'

'She said in the letter she'd wait another week before going to the doctor and then write to me again.' But he was convinced it was neither a false alarm nor a nabbing trick. Then I saw that, beyond the urge to flight, the affair brought satisfaction to him. Basically, he only dreaded a docking of his pay to support a child — all he could spare from it was posted home every week to his harassed mother.

He went back to camp that day, taking an afternoon train from Waterloo, his night's absence without leave earning C.B. punishment. All he had wanted, really, was exposition and support in his dilemma. He was twenty-one at the time. And Maureen's own dilemma turned out not to be false. Back in London by then, Caerphilly Jones was depressed but not distraught; the coming expense fretted him most. Yet a pearly dawn lay within his muddle. Taken to meet Maureen's parents for the matter to be thrashed out, he was approved by them, and, after lengthy negotiations, the mattress-maker succeeded in buying him out of the army. It was purchase of not only a son-in-law but of a trainee for the family business and a driver for the delivery van. Maureen was their sole offspring.

Distressed though the times were even in London, Caerphilly Jones did well for himself. People continued to get married despite the bad times, and mattresses remained an essential commodity. I was not invited to his wedding; my aid, such as it was, in bringing this about was to receive acknowledgement later. The wedding was a quiet, register-office affair, since by its date

Maureen, according to Caerphilly, looked like a 'full coaltruck'. Nobody came up from Wales for the wedding, either. Asked what he wanted for a wedding present, he said at once, 'A mirror for over the mantelpiece same as my mother's got,' and, after a moment, added, 'Or a *Pears' Cyclopaedia*. My auntie in Ynyshir used to have one.' I sold the George Grosz *Ecce Homo* I had bought in Germany, tracked down the type of mirror he wanted, and bought a *Pears*.

Almost a year elapsed before I met Mrs Jones, though Caerphilly continued to visit me regularly. She was brought to tea one Sunday afternoon. He stood at the door in the laurel hedge, slender Mrs Jones hovering behind at the iron gate. With a prim glance from under his lids, he deposited in my arms from his own a weighty baby in a wool wrap and frilly blue frock. 'Go on in, Maureen,' he urged, gave her a push, and returned to a small van standing drawn up by the gate. I had not ever carried a baby before. It was asleep. Inside my room, Maureen took it from me with a smile. Caerphilly came in, carrying a single-size mattress over his head. 'Brought you one of our best mattresses,' he said. 'I'll take your old one away in the van.' I did not need a new one. But it was a symbol of his swift rise to boss status.

Toasting Caerphilly cheese before the coal fire, as he had done off and on for three years except in high summer, its namesake complained that they only had gas-fires in their house. Sedate, with a quick Cockney liveliness hovering behind her reserve, his trim wife was very sure of herself within her own victory. There was not a grain of flightiness in her. In a year she had settled confidently into married life with her Welshman. She flowered into identification with the suddenly bawling child, and this was not applied to her husband. His manner with her, natural in the men of his native mining places, was non-uxurious and short-shrift in an acknowledging way. Wearing good week-end tweeds and smart brogues, he had a touch of strutting. He was a Welsh boy of the valleys who had made good in England. The mattress-making business employed five people; Maureen still worked at keeping her father's books, and she offered to do typing for me if I was stuck. Caerphilly had put on some weight. At the table he was no longer ravenous, as in the days when, despite all his eating, he remained lean and the insecurity in which he was bred had shed on him a lunar wildness.

He and Maureen had been down to Wales in the van to meet his family, taking the baby with them. 'It was seeing all the idle miners on street corners made it look so foreign,' Maureen observed. 'Hanging about for hours. We've got unemployment in London, but there's nothing else down there. The Depression is the right name for it. I felt all of me was squeezed down into my cold feet.'

'It's the means test bastards they can't stand,' Caerphilly said indignantly. 'Snouting into people's houses, asking questions. Anybody would think it's a test for consumption or the clap. I send my Mum postal orders regular and she's frightened to cash them in the post office down the road and goes by bus all the way to Pontypridd to do it. If the means test bloke finds out she's getting a pound from me he'd smack her fanny.'

'You got out of that place in time,' Maureen said, giving the gurgling child a spoonful of tea.

'Out of the frying-pan into the frigging army,' the father remarked. He pursed his lips as he looked down at his contribution to social order in his wife's arm. 'I liked the army,' he murmured, vaguely perverse.

'You were a silly and lovely soldier,' Maureen allowed him his flaunted plume. She rocked the child to sleep. I saw that, like me, she had recognized Caerphilly's quality and had made up her mind to view any blemishes with tolerance.

I had another look at the child and thought I detected Caerphilly's perfection of dark Iberian features. I wondered if the father would inherit the mattress business in the fullness of time. Maureen was teaching him the elements of book-keeping and other office routines. Who could have foreseen that he would end as a soldier? Kept on the Reserve list after the purchased release from his seven years' term, he was to be called up in 1939, and he did not return from battle.

Eight: The Charities

Rain streaked my arrival. Not the full mountainous works of windy torrents into which bulky Mrs Blow used to advance backwards from her pear-tree house to do her shopping up in the main street, but, as if in decent unison with the times, a slow falling of piano drops, going on and on. I climbed the hill. In the spattered gloom of an autumn evening huddled groups of men in old raincoats and pulled-down caps looked long spent of arguments and jests. Most of them were too elderly to ever venture beyond the mountain ramparts. They stopped on the street corners.

Ten shillings left in the bank, to keep my account open, I was arriving appropriately in the Rhondda. A wolf had been scratching at my green door in the laurel hedge, its warning howl clearly enunciating 'Commissioners of Inland Revenue'. I had got into a practice of flinging the taxmen's buff envelopes unopened into my rubbish bin. In one I had opened I found they had made their own ridiculous assessment of my earnings. The true earnings were so meagre that it had not seemed worthwhile making my returns. Besides, in the past nobody had told me that I could claim on professional expenses such as rent of a workplace, a telephone, typing and other items, and for some years, when I had declared my slender earnings, I had paid whatever tax was demanded.

Now, like Caerphilly Jones, I thought I could hide among the Welsh mountains. Also, I had a book to write, and I knew I would be fed and kept warm for the winter. (My flight from London was to turn out to be bootless, however; the taxmen gazed into their crystal, pursued, and my father paid the merciless sum.) I had given up my attractive studio and bunked. There had come a day when there just wasn't any of those round pieces of metal, to say nothing of those resplendent currency notes. Such times bring Job into one's bed during the long, dark, tossing hours. Cheques are due to arrive, and, dilatory as redemption at the hand of God, they never, never come at the proper time. Borrow? It stuck in my gullet. Besides, I had learnt that to lend money means almost certain loss of a friend.

But I hadn't been as bereft and despairing as an acquaintance of mine in London. A young actor insufficiently equipped with the necessary gruesome egotism of his profession, without which its pleasure-giving members cannot inflate themselves for projection across those treacherous footlights, he had come from New Zealand to conquer the London stage. For a while he found some ill-paid jobs in the many hole-and-corner club theatres of the Thirties. He wanted to collaborate with me in writing a play. A girl we both knew pined in love for him. She telephoned me one day after returning from a holiday and told me his fate. The actor hadn't been seen in his usual haunts for a fortnight or so. Either a sixth or the nasal sense of another lodger in a shabby bed-sitter house off Praed Street, to which the landlord went once a month for his rents, led to the forcing of a door. The actor was sitting in a chair. He had starved himself to death.

That laborious suicide could be apprehended — the initial steely resolution slowly easing into a dark ecstasy of total withdrawal from reality, far-off tappings of visitors on a locked door rid of the vanity of temptation. The actor's shattered girl adorer could see the tragedy only as the pride of refusal to dump himself on friends for meals, refusal to ask, ask, ask, to spurn the stiff-upperlip idiocy, to refuse to be one of the many parasites, often amusing, who made an evening at rowdy pubs like the Fitzroy so expensive. She said that every bite of food she took tasted of him. He had been hurried into a pauper's grave before she heard of the death. Every Sunday she took flowers to the numbered mound of Kensal Green earth.

> Oh, who sits weeping on my grave
> And will not let me sleep?

Charities, I found, were active in the Rhondda Valley. There were welfare settlements run by local authorities and the ever-modest Quakers in rented villas, institutional buildings and sheds. For a penny-a-week subscription you could play dominoes, get a cup of tea, rehearse for 'dramatics', be taught carpentry and house decoration. Thirty per cent of the employable colliers were permanently out of work that autumn, every week the number increased, and the lucky ones were on short time. The revenue of one coal-exporting Glamorgan docks had declined from £543,530 in 1929 to £46,680 in 1935. The pubs were quiet as the chapels. This was not the roaring Rhondda in which I had grown up. The battle of the pioneers was done: or at least had come to a nasty halt.

Calling on a Clydach Vale woman I had known, the headmistress of an infants' school, I found only her upper half visible above stacks and cartons of old clothes in her parlour. A London charity organization dispatched bales of discarded garments regularly to her home. Anybody unemployed in her area could call and state his or her needs. 'Do you want a pullover?' she asked, tossing me a Fair Isle woolly in reasonably good condition. Although as an author I wasn't eligible in an official sense, I accepted the charity; in Wales almost nobody sticks to the letter of English laws and decrees.

Children's garments predominated in Miss G's parlour. There were quantities of the long, woollen underpants men wore in bygone days; attic chests must have been turned out. Nearly everything else was woollen too. It seemed to display a touching belief that in places such as the Rhondda warmth was required. But there was a tattered evening gown of white satin and diamanté, its former splendour gone limp and grimy, all the shine out of it. 'Who on earth will wear this?' I asked, picking it up.

'It will do for the Dramatic Society,' Miss G said. 'They're putting on a play by Noel Coward this winter.'

A collier's wife, elderly and roundly fat, came in while I was there. I recalled seeing her long ago in my father's shop; she might have been an old debt in his Ledger of Old Accounts. She pounced on the men's long underpants. 'Shorter ones I want for my Ieuan,' she kept saying, measuring pairs against her own sturdy thigh. 'Is everybody in England tall as a lamp-post? But there's good quality!' Saying she could shorten them, she chose three pairs of the streamingly long garments, and turned to me, 'You won't remember the days when men used to wear those Welsh flannel underpants with tapes to tie below the knee, will you, Mr Davies *bach*? Striped they were, bright stripes.' She gurgled, her eyes still juicy. 'My Ieuan married me in a pair — had blue serge trousers over them, of course — and when we went to Porthcawl for a bit of a honeymoon I was surprised to see them because it was August and boiling hot. His mother it was made him wear them all the time. Brought up in the country, Merioneth way.' Such underpants were before my time, but I could well remember the fanged childhood shirts of Welsh flannel, fresh-washed for Sunday, and tough as our theology.

Ieuan's spirited wife left with the pants and a wool tam o'shanter for a neighbour's child. Miss G, her latest Aladdin consignment of bales and cartons piled around her, sighed as she looked out of her window at the dusky mountains. 'It all makes me feel there's a sinking ship out there,' she said. 'A ship of old people. I seem to be always writing character references for girls taking jobs as servants in England. I can't bear to let them go, after knowing them as infants in my school. Yet they ought to go.'

I went on that evening to a public meeting in Judges Hall, down in Tonypandy. It had been called to discuss and encourage a forthcoming Hunger March to London, due to start before deep winter set in. Plenty of young men were present. Also, unexpectedly, many women; these no longer kept their social concerns privately at their hearths in the tight, lengthy terraces of minute dwellings — how small they looked to me now! — streaking the lower mountain slopes. There was an atmosphere of active interest in the meeting. Yet no fire or smouldering ran in the proceedings. The two youngish speakers on the platform had none of the oratorical fervour of bygone miners' leaders; none of the rousing shoots into rhetorical clouds; no torpedoes speeding to their mark.

They made their comments with an ironical humour shorn of chagrin and bitterness. My hour in the hall brought to mind a death of old beliefs, with new ones not yet born. There was no especial contempt for the behaviour of two ratepayers who had instituted legal action against the Labour-dominated Council for granting £30 towards the expenses of the hunger march; taken to High Court, the case had been won by the ratepayers and £150 costs awarded against the Council. The references made on the platform to this typical Stanley Baldwin-like kick were weary. But the march would go on, as planned. Each marcher would need one blanket, an overcoat, a change of underclothes, at least three pairs of socks, an enamel plate, cup, knife and fork, and a valise or knapsack. First-aid accessories and musical instruments would be provided. Anyone could join, but I gathered that women were not expected to be tempted. It was nearly two hundred road miles to London.

A crayoned poster hung from a table on the platform. It announced a future event: *Who is to be Beauty Queen of the Rhondda? Prize Competition for Best-Looking Girl and Finest Ankles.* A famous boxer, born in the Rhondda, was to judge this difficult competition of gazelle ankles and rainwashed peach faces. The prize wasn't stated; going by what I had experienced of Welsh ability in formal organizing, it would be forgotten until an hour before adjudication, when a tea-cosy or box of apostle spoons would be fished out of somebody's old wedding presents in a chest of drawers.

It was the season of rain. Rain was falling when I left Judges Hall. Tier above tier, the dark terraces rose behind the main road, where enormous out-of-scale buses had replaced the slender tramcars of my childhood. Enraged elephants bumping up and down the jagged valley, the double-decker buses tilted round sharp corners, stampeded over steep drops. The old people did not like these snorting buses which were liable to shoot off at a tangent; when a tramcar stopped it stopped properly, silent and dignified on its rails, and at a lift of the hand it stopped anywhere, like a friend. I hankered for the graceful whippet vessels myself. As I took an aimless walk through the back tiers of ill-lit wet streets, a verse from a poem I had picked up somewhere ran through my head:

> When close as prison-bars, from overhead
> The sky lets fall the curtains of the rain,
> And voiceless hordes of spiders come, to spread
> Their shameful cobwebs through our darkened brains ...

The cubist terraces were diminished. As always, they escaped real squalor. The mountain air and winds cleansed, the rains washed. Chrysanthemums and evergreen bushes swayed where there were front gardens, doorsteps were 'scotched' white, strong ferns and fancy greenstuff sprang on interior window-sills. Inside a terraced block of fifty identical dwellings as many unidentical dramas or comedies were enacted at some time or other, similar only in a basic urgency. Each poky dwelling contained its thimbleful of dynamite; at some time in the long boring years of obedience to decent custom it would explode, and the moment of explosion was the flower I sought. But there was a decline and a diminishing now. The dreary economic struggle had gone on for so long! Was it lost? Had the wheel come full circle in this ever-worsening time of dole? Had coal lost its supreme might? Those stale charity clothes in Miss G's parlour! And that wretched Hunger March to an alien capital! At Marble Arch one Sunday afternoon, a couple of months earlier, I had seen mounted police, switches in action, charge into a turbulent crowd of marchers from a North of England area which was as miserably distressed as this Rhondda.

> And through my brain old hearses now advance
> In silence, always: Hope, so beautiful,
> Weeps her defeat, and conquering Anguish plants
> His great black banner on my cowering skull.

Yet from such miniature dwellings as these had come a whiff of future national triumphs. Who in Judges Hall that evening could have foretold the date of nationalization of Viscount Rhondda's Cambrian Combine? Or of the Welfare State schemes? I remembered the sound of a summoning bugle when I woke from sleep just before a dawn, remembered the secret tramp of feet advancing to the colliery powerhouse in Clydach Vale, remembered our country servant dashing out among rioters to rescue her brother from police batons, remembered the troops with their bayonets, and the charity soup kitchens for children, and my ever-hungry schoolfriend, Jim Reilly, wishing the bloody strikes would last for ever.

My father's shop looked diminished too. Since we no longer lived on the premises, I visited it like a customer, for a single melancholy occasion. There was a sulky girl assistant whose ex-collier young man had fled the place and did not write to her. Our horse and cart had long since gone; a boy delivered by handtruck such heavy orders as there were. But the stout black ledger of old debts lay on the sloped desk of frosted glass. Gone was the funnelled coffee-grinding machine that had breathed a robust odour of welcome. Dried fruits, rice, tea and other safeties of life were in ready-made cartons, replacing the Monday hand-packaging in coloured paper bags. Gone too was our most obstreperous woman customer, Mrs Hughes Number 8, who used to sway across the road on Saturday nights from the dark pub-cave of pickled women, and declare, as she bought large quantities of bacon and cheese, 'I've got eight men and a husband to feed'. She had joined the son she had lost, her youngest, whose walking funeral was the first I attended. Also gone, though not dead, was the elegant Gentleman Collier of the coloured velvet jackets and Renaissance coiffure, on whose behalf my exasperated mother had brought her day-book down on to the head of the drunken collier who rudely challenged him. The Gentleman Collier had retreated to a country paradise in England and launched into market-gardening with a friend.

In this skeleton time my father sometimes referred in aggrieved tones to my mother's refusal to abandon this unreliable valley when, long ago, he had been offered a bargain-priced pub in the up-and-coming seaside town of Porthcawl, then an unravished bride of quietness. Yet it was she who from the beginning had distrusted these mining valleys of eternal strife and millstone ledgers of debts. 'No child of mine is going to be brought up in a public house,' she had said, thus depriving me of inheritance. Reversing the religious position at home, too, my formerly agnostic father, who had placed all his faith in rugby teams, cricket and golf, had now become a faithful member of St Thomas's church, and my mother ceased to attend the Welsh chapel where I had itched in an evil flannel shirt on Sundays.

My calling did not entitle my joining the swarms of Friday dole-receivers at Tonypandy unemployment exchange. And I lived in some comfort; my parents could afford to provide my abbreviated requirements. A novel about a mining valley pub which I was writing, called *Jubilee Blues*, took this and that from the elegiac proceedings around me. 'Change and decay in all around I see' became my lugubrious burden. There were far too many items for use in the microcosm of my pub.

Continued family and tribal loyalties brought a sense of native tenacity enduring within the valley ramparts. I heard that the town council of a coastal place had decided that a brass band and park bandstand would help buttress local morale. Out of the horde of applicants for the post of band conductor a blood relation of the mayor found himself on the short list, travelled down from one of the blighted inner valleys, and faced the selection committee in the council chamber with proper nervous respect. 'Well now, Mr Cymmer,' the mayor blew encouragingly across his desk, 'what is the music you know, *bach*?' His jumpy eye cast on the babbling other committee members sitting around with their feet up, Mr Cymmer confused the Welsh term of endearment with something else: 'Bach? Why now, when he came to Builth eisteddfod last year we went walking together after the chief choral. Know him and his works better than my own trombone.' 'Beethoven?' nodded the mayor, ignoring the more disinterested conversation going on among his colleagues. 'Beethoven?' caught Mr Cymmer. 'Met him in the Crystal Palace up in London two times. Said he'd be coming down one day to see me and Gwyneth the wife.' 'Shut up, you lot,' bawled the mayor to his committee. 'A bunch of gossiping old women .... Right'o, Mr Cymmer, off with you. You'll be having a letter.' Envied by many, and maligned by few, Mr Cymmer moved down to the town, dressed his sparetime band in gold-braided uniform, and was a pit-haulier on the dole no more. The item was typical enough to be true.

Before the winter had advanced I walked over thick mountains to a neighbouring valley in search of Caerphilly Jones's family. Several of these small, tucked-away valleys, each with its colliery, had flourished in self-contained privacy outside the Rhondda, metropolis of them all. From a mountain brow, this one looked like a peaceful kraal. Its single-shaft colliery, sunk late in the nineteenth century, had not ever been run by a company; the founder boss had also owned the terraces of dwellings and the shops, and there were tales of *droit de seigneur* babies and other period lordlinesses.

Autumnal tints lingered in the trough below me, a stream of copper mountain water ran through, lazy threads of smoke came from chimneys of the hut-like dwellings. There was no railway station, though a track for coaltrucks ran to the valley's sky-arched opening. Low on the opposite mountain slope were several 'levels' — primitive holes running deep into the flank, from which inferior coal had been disgorged. One of them had been opened up again in these bad times. At its entrance I could see three men, troglodytes in the distance, filling a sack. It all suggested a Breughel painting of eternal peasant occupations in a remote time.

I descended, and presently knocked on a door opening direct

on a rough pavement, one of forty or so doors in a terrace of untrimmed stone. In which of the adjacent dwellings had the old granny potted a pineapple for her front window-sill? A very large woman, massive arms bulging from a puce cardigan with rolled-up sleeves, opened the door and completely filled its space. Barring my entrance to her citadel, she eyed me with Boadicean hostility, ferocious words ready to punch out of her extensive jaws. It would have taken a battering-ram manned by six Romans to remove her from her portal. No doubt she thought the stranger was another means test man or some other State intruder. When I explained who I was, she ejaculated, 'I'm his Mam! Come in, come in. He told me you would be coming some day .... Gethin,' she shrieked down the tiny passage behind her, 'fill the kettle.'

She was doing her duty by the son I had nicknamed Caerphilly. But there was something shattering about her; she looked an unreliable woman of vindictive temper, a fighter in the wrong way, a wagonload of heaving flesh devoid of jollity. Her little eyes shifted about and pounced. In the slovenly back room, its dull fireplace unraked for days, there was an odour of dirt and old cushions on a filthy settee. Caerphilly's brother, a weedy boy of twelve, gave me an uninterested glance, put a tin kettle on the dull coals and returned to a jigsaw puzzle on the table. 'My husband will be coming in a minute, I expect,' Mrs Jones shouted. 'Gone down to the Recreation. Have you got a fag on you?' She eyed me as I gave her a cigarette, summing me up, suspicion ready. 'Come from Clydach Vale, have you?' What was I after? I felt I had made a mistake in coming.

'I walked over the mountains.'

'*Walked*, did you!' Dubiousness of me was plain. Why hadn't I, who had lived in London, come in a car? Was I poor too? 'Well,' she said, 'it'll soon be too dark for you to go back over the mountains, boyo. There's a bus passing the Spout every hour. My husband will take you to the pub down there if you want.' I knew then that I ought to have brought a bottle.

She made tea in a smeared brown pot. I talked of Caerphilly. 'He sends me a bit of money regular,' his mother declared, 'but, Duw, Duw, it's never enough. He must be doing well for himself, bought out of the army like that! They came here in a van. *She's* a tidy piece, I thought, but I wouldn't have chosen her — not on the whole, I wouldn't. Nothing much in her. He could have done better for himself in London, I said to myself.'

I sipped my strong tea, into which she had dropped a spoonful of condensed milk out of a tin. I was surprised. Surely she knew about the improper pregnancy? She went on to say that they had brought a new mattress down in the van, but she didn't like those hard mattresses, only feather ones, so she sold it to the publican's wife. Her talk ran on values and money. The door-latch clicked, and a short, thin man in a cap entered. He, too, darted a hostile look at the stranger on the settee as he went immediately into a lean-to scullery. I had caught a flea by then, which darted around the small of my back. Mrs Jones took at least a minute to explain my presence to her scowling husband.

His comparative smallness astonished me; a limp whip of a man, he reached to his wife's shoulder. He grunted a few remarks, but no direct gazing came from eyes that had the wet red glisten of pomegranate seeds. He bore not the slightest resemblance to the graceful, neat and handsome Caerphilly. Neither did the gigantic woman who had clumsily dropped an open tea-caddy, spilling all the contents, so that we drank tea made of leaves scooped up from the dirty rag hearth-mat. Mrs Jones produced a huge slab of over-sweet factory cake wedged with a green and white concoction. Gethin ate a lot of it, and said not a word over his jigsaw, which had come from the welfare centre. He had no likeness to his brother, either.

Caerphilly, I decided, was a throwback to some more splendid ancestry, a reminder of an old racial sumptuousness. Or was there a *droit de seigneur* history, of more recent date? Perhaps, in her way, his mother had detected this special quality and that was why she had expressed dissatisfaction with his ordinary marriage. I had seen examples of such atavism before in one or two deteriorated families of the old breed. A sparkling creature appeared, usually male, disconnected from the others, the immortal stranger at the gate. If there was an endowment of brain as well, which was even rarer, a superb human being was born. Caerphilly seemed to have little brain power. Or had all the circumstances of his upbringing been an obliteration?

The flea bit me. I wanted to scratch and shake myself. I wanted to go. My visit seemed meaningless. Mr Jones calculated me sideways, like an untrustworthy mongrel. Was he wondering if I could be touched for a quid? He told me he'd been unemployed for five years. All he could run to now was one pint of beer a week; in the old days he'd drink a dozen on Fridays and Saturdays. He kept a pigeon cote down the backyard and, glad of the opportunity to shake myself, I went with him to see the dapper birds. I said I had to be home early, couldn't go to the pub, and I slipped him ten shillings for drinks, all I could afford. Mrs Jones saw me to the front door. 'Are you strict with him?' she said, meaning Caerphilly. 'You've got to be strict with that one.' I couldn't think what she meant. I only remembered he had sent her a postal order every week out of his miserable soldier's pay.

Her great fist of a head, colossal torso, arms and legs, blocked the door again. I had a fugitive vision of her swelling until she cracked and demolished the walls of the bantam dwelling, her head breaking out of the slate roof. She was a dangerous force of handicapped life, without co-ordination at present. In other circumstances she would be among those women who bawled around the guillotine or defended barricades. I thought of the episode in Welsh history when Pembroke women had banded together in scarlet cloaks and witch hats to meet French invaders and, yelling on a cliff-top, frightened the intruders back to their ships. A pandemonium within this descendant had been reduced to a meanness. Had it come from the vast levelling-down of an impersonal industrialism that in its present ruin degraded yet provided some wherewithal for a wretched existence? Their investigating snouts quivering with a sharper intelligence than the French invaders had possessed, it was means test men who poked into the sacred privacies of these dwellings now.

My flea seemed to have left me. I hurried towards the crossroads for my bus at the valley's mouth. There were a few paltry shops in the main road, a plain chapel, a school, a pub, and not a person to be seen. The evening was closing in. No lights gleamed in the terrace windows. Caerphilly's father had said that the colliery had shut down completely three years before, though there was always talk that it would be reopened. This was still a half-rural valley, but there was none of the eternal rhythm of the old, hard, dependable farming life; only a few pigsties and poultry shacks. In this mongrel place and in this dead interim all the social wars seemed to be lost, as empty year followed empty year meaninglessly.

My bus swooped away from the elementary coign, swore its way down dark bends, bumped at length into the Rhondda. My flea hadn't gone. Rewarmed into venom in the bus, it bit my hip and, the size of a camel, speeded to other quarters fast as a drop of quicksilver. The only other time I had been so harried by a flea was in the packed cheapest seats of the Albert Hall. It had been as virulent an insect then, active right through Melba's final Sunday afternoon encore of *Home, Sweet Home*, the vocalist removing her flashing diamond rings to accompany herself at the piano. I jumped off the bus at Penygraig, found a dark back lane, dropped my trousers and flapped my shirt. The flea went.

Well, I had picked up a flea in a poverty-stricken hovel I had chosen to visit. My own poverty was on a different scale. In my parents' house I had a comfortable room for work on my novel, I had pleasing food, and I paid nothing. I was another kind of parasite. I settled into the dismal winter, going out less and less. The solitary occupant of a lighthouse, or a spider weaving a web in the rafters, I had one of the loneliest jobs in the world. It was also self-chosen. There was not a bounden duty for anyone else to pay the slightest attention. The long wallowing in introspection brought cantankerousness, phobias, cold feet, neurosis, and saintliness. I starved vicariously and was conscious of the discomfort of a halo. I could not bring myself to accept money for work until it was done. A firm of publishers, Putnams, had offered me a fixed quarterly sum on the undertaking that I produced a novel a year for three years, but I resisted the temptation. T.M. Ragg, the sensitive younger director, advised me too not to accept the offer if I could possibly hold out.

Three or four pounds for back royalties turned up and I blew the lot on a reduced-price Saturday train excursion to London, where I wanted to see a production of Chekhov's *The Seagull*. The beloved Russian sorcerer worked his spell. In Constantine I saw some of my own plight, though I was impatient of the final-curtain conventionality of his suicide, and D.H. Lawrence's exasperating jeer of Chekhov being a 'piddling Willy wet-leg' was valid for a moment. I returned on the midnight train from Paddington, with a long brooding wait on punishing Cardiff station for my milk-churns connexion to the Rhondda, and, as on an occasion in my stout boyhood, again I was the only passenger for the region of rainy mountain winds, tears, hunger marches, bigger unemployment figures, and much else.

Acknowledgements

Part of my sketch of Dr William Price's life, 'A Drop of Dew', first appeared in *The Mint*, a miscellany edited by Geoffrey Grigson, and part of my memoir of D.H. Lawrence, 'The Bandol Phoenix', in *Horizon*, edited by Cyril Connolly. Acknowledgements are also made to the Humanities Research Center of the University of Texas, Laurence Pollinger Limited and the Estate of the late Mrs Frieda Lawrence for permission to quote from letters to me from D.H. and Frieda Lawrence; to John Baker Ltd (The Richards Press) for a quotation from a poem by Anna Wickham (Mrs Edith Hepburn); to Professor Gwyn Williams for a few lines of translation from the sixth-century Welsh of Llywarch Hen; and to an untraceable translator of a Baudelaire poem. I would like also to express my indebtedness to R. Page Arnot's authoritative history, *South Wales Miners* (Allen & Unwin, 1967) for refreshing my childhood memories of brave Rhondda valley battles.

R.D.

About Simon Baker

Simon Baker is a lecturer in the English Department at University of Wales Swansea, He specializes in twentieth-century British fiction, particularly the modern short story. He has published numerous articles and reviews, and he coordinates the unique Master's Degree course on Welsh writing in English offered at Swansea.